Colloquial Arabic of Egypt

The Colloquial Series

* Colloquial Arabic (Levantine)
* Colloquial Arabic of the Gulf and Saudi Arabia
* Colloquial Chinese
  Colloquial Czech
  Colloquial Dutch
* Colloquial English
  Colloquial French
  Colloquial German
  Colloquial Greek
  Colloquial Hungarian
  Colloquial Italian
  Colloquial Japanese
  Colloquial Persian
* Colloquial Polish
  Colloquial Portuguese
  Colloquial Romanian
  Colloquial Russian
* Colloquial Serbo-Croat
  Colloquial Spanish
  Colloquial Turkish

* Accompanying cassette available

Colloquial Arabic
of Egypt

Russell H. McGuirk

Routledge & Kegan Paul
London, Boston and Henley

First published in 1986
by Routledge & Kegan Paul plc

14 Leicester Square, London WC2H 7PH, England

9 Park Street, Boston, Mass. 02108, USA and

Broadway House, Newtown Road,
Henley on Thames, Oxon RG9 1EN, England

Phototypeset in Linotron Times 9 on 11 pt
by Input Typesetting Ltd, London
and printed in Great Britain
by Cox and Wyman
Reading, Berks

Library of Congress Cataloging in Publication Data

McGuirk, Russell H., 1946–
Colloquial Arabic of Egypt.
(Colloquial series)
Bibliography: p.
1. Arabic language—Dialects—Egypt—Grammar.
I. Title.
PJ6779.M43 1985 492'.77'0962 85–2247

British Library Cataloguing in Publication Data also available

ISBN 0–7100–9936–3 (pb)
0–7102–0581–3 (cass)

CONTENTS

ACKNOWLEDGMENTS

Thanks are due to my Egyptian friends and colleagues Nagdi Madbouli Ibrahim, Hosni Abdul Aal, and Fat'hy Farouk for their unstinting help in answering my questions about the fine points of their native language; to Mahmoud Said Mansour who, in addition to checking the earlier lessons, provided the Goha stories and proverbs; and to Professor F. H. Megally, who kindly went over the finished manuscript.

The reading passage 'il-itneen ahmadaat' is adapted from a broadcast of the *kilmiteen wi-bass* series by Fouad El-Mohandis, and is included by the kind permission of the Egyptian Radio and TV Union.

Finally, thanks are also due to *Al-Ahram* newspaper for their permission to reproduce Salah Gahin's cartoon, which appears on page 94.

INTRODUCTION

The purpose of this handbook is to introduce the Colloquial – or 'spoken' – Arabic of Egypt. Specifically, it aims to provide easy access to the Arabic which Egyptians, particularly the educated of Cairo and Alexandria, learn in the home and use in everyday life.

It is important to realise that spoken Arabic differs considerably from written Arabic. The Arabs call their written language **fúṣHa** or 'pure'; this volume refers to it in English as Classical Arabic.* It will suffice to mention here that Classical Arabic is the same for Arabs everywhere and that they learn it in school, much as Europeans once learned Latin for literary and formal purposes.

Egyptians call Colloquial Arabic **il-lúgha d-dáariga**, which means 'the common language'.** Two important features are: that it is hardly ever written except for modern theatre scripts and cartoon captions; and that it differs from country to country. The forms of Colloquial Arabic spoken in Morocco, Egypt, Lebanon and Iraq represent distinct and quite different dialects, though in fact it would be difficult to find clear boundaries to divide one dialect from another. Colloquial Arabic changes almost imperceptibly from town to town, and usually becomes clearly different only with distance.

Egyptian Arabic is generally understood by Arabs everywhere. It is the colloquial form spoken natively by about a third of all Arabs and is therefore the most widely used of the dialects. Moreover, its stature among the dialects is further enhanced by the fact that Egyptians play a leading cultural role in exporting their films, TV programmes, and popular songs – in their own dialect – as entertainment for the entire Arab World.

One should not consider any important aspect of Egyptian life without some mention of history. Certainly the forces that caused Egyptian Arabic to evolve from the kind of Arabic spoken by the Arab army that conquered Egypt in AD 639 are of historical interest evoking, as they do, names like Ibn Tulun, the Sultan

*Other English names are Modern Literary Arabic and Modern Standard Arabic.

Or **il-lúgha el-9ammíyya, which means the same thing.

Selim, Saladin, Baibars, the Mamelukes, and Napoleon. Through fourteen centuries Arabic has had to jostle first with the native Coptic, and then with the native languages of new but non-Arab invaders – Kurdish, Turkish, Albanian, French, and (not least!) English. You, as a student of Egyptian Arabic, will soon see for yourself that what has made turbulent history has also resulted in a most colourful and expressive language.

THE TAPE

There is an optional cassette accompanying the book. A considerable amount of the Arabic material has been recorded. This is marked ■ in the text.

PRONUNCIATION

The correct pronunciation of some of these letters, for example ح and ع, it is scarcely possible for a European to acquire, except by long intercourse with natives.

A Grammar of the Arabic Language (1859)
by W. Wright

The problems of mastering Arabic pronunciation have often been greatly exaggerated. The truth is that the various sounds which you as a beginner are about to encounter, some of which are undeniably 'exotic', are not all that difficult so long as you *hear* the sounds in question, and do not rely solely on written descriptions. If you cannot find a 'native' to help you, you may use the cassette that has been especially prepared to accompany this volume. You should realise the degree to which good pronunciation is the key to success in the study of any new language. Without it a good grasp of grammar and vocabulary can seem pointless. The corollary is that with good pronunciation habits even a beginner, possessing only the rudiments of grammar and a small vocabulary, will be impressive.

WARNING: Do not assume that learning Egyptian Arabic is easier if approached through the Arabic alphabet. Quite the opposite! The Arabic alphabet suits Classical Arabic perfectly, but the sounds of Egyptian Arabic are actually more easily and efficiently represented by Latin letters. Nevertheless, learning the Arabic alphabet can obviously enrich your study of the language and if you are tempted you may refer to the table of Arabic letters given at the end of this introductory section.

The system of transliteration set out below is purely phonetic – that is, each symbol represents only one sound.

VOWELS

The two-lettered symbols are the long vowels and diphthongs. They have about twice the duration of short vowels, i.e. the single-lettered symbols.

symbol	*English equivalent*
a	(i) the *a* in *at*
	(ii) the first *a* in *aha*!*
aa	(i) the *a* in *man*
	(ii) the *a* in *far**
i	the *i* in *bit*
ii	the *ee* in *deep*
u	the *u* in *pull*
uu	the *oo* in *pool*
e	a short clipped *e* as in *bet*
o	a short clipped *o* as in *yo-ho-ho*
ee (a diphthong)	the *ay* in *day*
oo (a diphthong)	the *o* in *open*

Pronunciation exercise 1

aa	áalif	('alif', an Arabic letter)
a	alf	(a thousand)
ii	miin	(who?)
i	min	(from)
uu	fuul	(fava beans)
u	full	(jasmine)
ee	beet	(house)
e	bétna	(our house)
oo	yoom	(day)
o	yoméen	(two days)

CONSONANTS

The following Egyptian consonants have approximate English equivalents.

b as in English
d pronounced forward in the mouth like the *d* in *dental*

*The quality of vowels, particularly 'a' and 'aa', is influenced by the proximity of an emphatic consonant [the emphatics are introduced later in the pronunciation section]. This means that where one or more emphatic consonants occur in a word, both 'a' and 'aa' are pronounced as in the second alternatives given for each above.

f	as in English
g	always hard like the *g* in *go*
h	like the *h* in *house*
k	as in English
l	pronounced forward in the mouth like the *l* in *late*
m	as in English
n	as in English
p	as in English (foreign words only)*
s	like the *s* in *soup*
š	like the *sh* in *ship*
t	pronounced forward in the mouth like the *t* in *tea*
v	as in English (foreign words only)
w	like the *w* in *wolf*
y	like the *y* in *yet*
z	like the *z* in *zebra*
ž	like the *s* in *measure*

The following Egyptian consonants have no English equivalents:

gh	a vibrating gh sound like that made by gargling; like the *r* in French
H	a strong H pronounced with a rush of air from the throat. Pretend you are trying to blow out a flame with an H sound
q	a *k* sound pronounced far back in the throat
r	a slightly trilled *r* as in Spanish and Italian
'	the so-called 'glottal stop', which is the stop in the middle of 'uh-oh' or in the Cockney word 'bo''le' (for bottle). This symbol is also used at the beginning of a word to indicate that its first letter was originally q, no longer pronounced. Anywhere else in a word it might represent either this suppressed q or the hamza of Classical Arabic (see p. 9)
9	the sound made when the throat muscles are clenched. Try to swallow the sound 'ah'. When you sound as if you are being strangled, you will have mastered the 'voiced pharyngeal fricative'!

*The *p* is rather difficult for Arabs to pronounce. You will often hear Egyptians pronounce it as *b*, e.g. 'in for a benny, in for a bound'

Pronunciation exercise 2

g	gaar, agáaza, talg	(neighbour, holiday, ice)
ž	žiláati, garažáat, beež	(ice-cream, garages, beige)
gh	gharb, šughl, dimáagh	(west, work, brain)
h	hináak, gáahiz, nabíih	(there, ready, intelligent)
H	Halwáan, fatáaHa, ruuH	(Helwan, opener, go!)
k	kaam, ráakib, sabbáak	(how much, riding, plumber)
q	qur'áan, aqsáam, yiqáarin	(Koran, departments, compare)
r	ṛáagil, árnab, naar	(man, rabbit, fire)
x	xábar, baxt, moxx	(news, luck, brains)
9	9áli, sáa9a, rugúu9	(Ali, hour, return)
'	di'íi'a, da'áayi', sáabi'	(minute, minutes, former)

The emphatic consonants are ḍ, ṣ, ṭ, ẓ. There are also emphatic versions of l and r, but these will only be marked emphatic before a long 'a' sound.

Emphatic letters sound thickened and heavy. Although they are not difficult, you must hear them correctly pronounced to get them right. Either ask a native Egyptian to help you or refer to the cassette recordings especially available to accompany this book.

Pronunciation exercise 3

non-emphatic	*emphatic*	
durg	ḍuhr	(drawer, back)
daas	ḍáani	(he trod, mutton)
saab	ṣaam	(he left (something), he fasted)
sahl	ṣabr	(easy, patience)
taar	ṭaar	(revenge, it (m.) flew)
zaad	ẓáabiṭ	(he increased, officer)
zayy	ẓann	(like, he was of the opinion)
Hisáab	Huṣáan	(account, horse)
bádla	béeḍa	(suit, egg)
baat	baaṭ	(he stayed the night, underarm)

másgid	maṣr	(mosque, Egypt)
ba9d	ba9ḍ	(after, some)
	aḷḷáah	(God)
	ṛaas	(head)

DOUBLED CONSONANTS

The general rule is that doubled consonants are prolonged to twice the duration of single consonants.

Pronunciation exercise 4

single	*doubled*	
buxáar	yi'áxxar	(steam, he delays)
dáwa	áwwil	(medicine, first)
ámal	ámma	(hope, as for)

Pronunciation exercise 5

Here are some colourful words and expressions to practise pronouncing:

báladi	*local, 'native'*
galabíyya	*galabia, traditional garment of male Egyptians*
yúusif afándi	*tangerines*
xawáaga	*foreign 'gentleman'*
in šaa' aḷḷáah	*God willing*
barsíim	*clover*
gámal	*camel*
ba'šíiš	*baksheesh*
9afríit	*demon, imp; mischievous child*
dáwša	*commotion, usually a shouting match in the street*
mašrabíyya	*old style projecting latticework window*
waḷḷáahi-l-9aẓíim	*By God! – a common oath*
ya rabb	*O Lord!*
ya ṛáagil	*O man*

fulúuka	*felucca, kind of Nile boat with lateen sail*
far9óoni	*Pharaonic*
zag͟hariit	*long trilling sound, usually of joy, made by Arab women, e.g., at weddings*
ṣa9íidi	*Upper Egyptian*
'íbṭi	*Coptic*
Hamáam	*pigeon*
Hammáam	*bath*
nayrúuz	*Coptic New Year*
mu'ázzin	*mu'ezzin, caller to prayer*
ṣaláaH id-diin	*Saladin*
9abd il-9azíiz	*Abdul Aziz*

and some place names:

xaan il-xalíili	*Khan al-Khalili, a Cairo bazaar*
il-qaahíra	*Cairo*
il-mu'áṭṭam	*Muqattam, hills to Cairo's east*
máari gírgis	*a Coptic church in Old Cairo*
šáari9 il-mu9ízz li-diin iḷḷaah	*a main street in Old Cairo*
il-azbakíyya	*Ezbekiyya, a quarter of Cairo*
it-tawfi'íyya	*Tawfikiyya, a quarter of Cairo*
iz-za'azíi'	*Zagazig, a town in the Delta*

THE ARABIC ALPHABET

(1 = beginning of word; 2 = middle; 3 = end of word; 4 = standing alone)

4	*3*	*2*	*1*	*Name*	*Classical pronunciation*	*Egyptian pronunciation*
ا	ـا			alif	*	*
ب	ـب	ـبـ	بـ	baa	b	b
ت	ـت	ـتـ	تـ	taa	t	t
ث	ـث	ـثـ	ثـ	thaa (*th*in)	th	t or s
ج	ـج	ـجـ	جـ	giim	j	g (hard)
ح	ـح	ـحـ	حـ	Haa	H	H
خ	ـخ	ـخـ	خـ	xaa	x	x
د	ـد	ـد	د	daal	d	d
ذ	ـذ	ـذ	ذ	thaal (*th*ose)	th	d or z
ر	ـر	ـر	ر	raa	r	r
ز	ـز	ـز	ز	zaay	z	z
س	ـس	ـسـ	سـ	siin	s	s
ش	ـش	ـشـ	شـ	šiin	š	š
ص	ـص	ـصـ	صـ	ṣaad	ṣ	ṣ
ض	ـض	ـضـ	ضـ	ḍaad	ḍ	ḍ
ط	ـط	ـطـ	طـ	ṭaa	ṭ	ṭ
ظ	ـظ	ـظـ	ظـ	ẓaa	ẓ	ẓ or ḍ
ع	ـع	ـعـ	عـ	9een	9	9
غ	ـغ	ـغـ	غـ	gheen	gh	gh
ف	ـف	ـفـ	فـ	faa	f	f
ق	ـق	ـقـ	قـ	qaaf	q	q or ’
ك	ـك	ـكـ	كـ	kaaf	k	k
ل	ـل	ـلـ	لـ	laam	l	l
م	ـم	ـمـ	مـ	miim	m	m
ن	ـن	ـنـ	نـ	nuun	n	n
ه	ـه	ـهـ	هـ	haa	h	h
و	ـو	ـو	و	waaw	w	w
ي	ـي	ـيـ	يـ	yaa	y	y

*alif is used (i) as a written symbol for the aa (long a) sound; and also (ii) to bear the hamza mark (e.g., أ), which signifies the glottal stop.

ROOT LETTERS AND GRAMMATICAL PATTERNS

Like other Semitic languages, Arabic is characterised by a system of triliteral roots, each of which indicates a 'concept'. In other words, the vast majority of Arabic words consist of three root letters embedded in a fixed pattern. These root letters indicate the general concept with which the word is associated, while the pattern gives the precise meaning within that general concept.

By way of example, consider the three consonants **KTB**, which signify the general idea of 'writing'. By putting these consonants into specific patterns Arabs derive all the words they need that have to do with the concept, in this case, of 'writing'. The pattern **CaaCiC** (where C = consonant) means the doer of the action, so **káatib** is the word for 'writer'. Similarly we have:

CiCaaC	=	**kitáab**	=	book
maCCaC	=	**máktab**	=	'office' or 'desk'
maCCuuC	=	**maktúub**	=	'written'

etc.

As you pursue your study of Arabic the consistency and predictability of the language will become increasingly obvious. You will begin to guess correctly the meanings of words you have never seen before just by recognising their root letters and patterns.

ABBREVIATIONS

m.	masculine
f.	feminine
s.	singular
pl.	plural
v.	verb
v.n.	verbal noun
n.	noun
adj.	adjective
adv.	adverb
c.	collective
trans.	transitive
intrans.	intransitive
o.s.	oneself
pers.	person
perf.	perfect
imperf.	imperfect
impera.	imperative
voc.	vocative
lit.	literally
s.o.	someone
s.th.	something
resp.	response
V	vowel
C	consonant
CA	Classical Arabic

LESSON ONE
(id-dars il-áwwil)

I COMMON EXPRESSIONS

1	saláamu 9aléekum	*Hello*
(resp.)	9aléekum is-saláam	*Hello*
2	ṣabáaH il-xeer	*Good morning*
(resp.)	ṣabáaH in-nuur	*Good morning*
3	izzáyyak? (to m.s.)	*How are you?*
or	izzáyyik? (to f.s.)	
or	izzayyúkum? (to pl.)	
(resp.)	kwáyyis, il-Hámdu lilláah (by m.s.)	*Fine, thank you*
or	kwayyísa, il-Hámdu lilláah (by f.s.)	
or	kwayyisíin, il-Hámdu lilláah (by pl.)	

Notes

By 'resp.' is meant the standard response to the preceding phrase. (1) A traditional formal greeting. Lit. = 'peace upon you' and (resp.) 'upon you peace'. The original CA expression is **is-saláamu 9aléekum** but Egyptians often drop the definite article from the opening phrase. **saláamu 9aléekum** may be used, for example: (i) when entering a room; (ii) passing an acquaintance in the hall or on the street; and (iii) to mean 'good-bye' (by the person departing). (2) Lit. = 'morning of goodness' and (resp.) 'morning of light'. Some pleasant variations to the response are **ṣabáaH il-ward** ('morning of roses') and **ṣabáaH il-full** ('morning of jasmine').
(3) **izzáay** means 'how' and **izzáyyak** 'how are you?' Other ways to say 'how are you?' are:

izzáay ṣiHHítak	lit. =	*'how is your* (m.) *health?'*
izzáay ṣiHHítik		*'how is your* (f.) *health?'*
izzáay ṣiHHítkum		*'how is your* (pl.) *health?'*

and:

izzáay iṣ-ṣíHHa	lit. =	*'how is the health?'*

Note also:

izzáay il-awláad	*'how are the children?'*
izzáay il-madáam	*'how is madam?'* (i.e. your wife)

kwáyyis is the usual word for 'good'. **kwayyísa** is the feminine, and **kwayyisíin** the plural.

il-Hámdu lilláah is a CA phrase used whenever something or someone is said to be good, in good health, or improving. Lit. = 'praise (be) to God'.

II GRAMMAR

The Definite Article

The definite article in Egyptian Arabic is **il-**. There is no indefinite article in Arabic.

beet	*house, a house*
il-beet	*the house*

Before certain consonants the **l** of the definite article is assimilated. These are **d, ḍ, n, r, s, ṣ, š, t, ṭ, z, ẓ** and (optionally) **g** and **k**.

	iṛ-ṛáagil	*the man*
	is-sitt	*the woman*
	il-gurnáan	
or	ig-gurnáan	*the newspaper*
	il-kitáab	
or	ik-kitáab	*the book*

Nouns and Gender

In Arabic nouns are either masculine or feminine. They are generally easy to differentiate. The best approach is to learn how to recognize feminine nouns, which include

(a) those which clearly refer to females
(b) the vast majority of nouns ending in **-a**

(c) most cities and countries
(d) certain parts of the body
(e) a small group of miscellaneous nouns
Nouns which do not fit in any of these categories are almost always masculine.

Some feminine nouns (by category)

a		b		c	
sitt	*woman, lady*	ṭaṛabéeza	*table*	iskindiríyya	*Alexandria*
bint	*girl, daughter*	ginéena	*garden*	maṣr	*Egypt, Cairo**
uxt	*sister*	madíina	*city*	landan	*London*
umm	*mother*	9arabíyya	*car*	ingiltíra	*England*

d		e	
ṛaas	*head*	šams	*sun*
9een	*eye*	Harb	*war*
iid	*hand*	aṛḍ	*land*
rigl	*foot, leg*	naar	*fire*

Some masculine nouns

ṛáagil	*man*	baab	*door*	gáami9	*mosque*
wálad	*boy, son*	muftáaH	*key*	máṭ9am	*restaurant*
axx	*brother*	šibbáak	*window*	'álam	*pen*
abb	*father*	šáari9	*street*	nahr	*river*
gurnáan	*newspaper*	beet	*house*	in-niil	*the Nile*
kúrsi	*chair*	kúbri	*bridge*	háram	*pyramid*
kitáab	*book*	sawwáa'	*driver*	baHr	*sea*
máktab	*office, desk*	midáan	*city square*	falláah	*farmer, peasant*

Plurals

Arabic plurals may be divided into 'sound plurals' which are regular and predictable; and 'broken plurals' which follow numerous unpre-

***il-qaahíra**, the CA word for 'Cairo', is also common.

dictable patterns. The masculine sound plural is made by adding the suffix **--iin** to the singular noun or adjective [cf. Lesson Two] and shortening any preceding long vowel.

falláaH	→ fallaHíin	*farmers, peasants*
sawwáa'	→ sawwa'íin	*drivers*

The feminine sound plural is made by adding the suffix **--aat** with a shortening of any preceding long vowel. This is the plural form for many nouns and some adjectives bearing the feminine ending **--a** in the singular. For these the **--aat** replaces the **--a**.

ṭaṛabéeza	→ ṭaṛabezáat	*tables*
9arabíyya	→ 9arabiyyáat	*cars*

Sometimes the feminine sound plural ending occurs together with some structural change to the single form of the noun. Notice the illogical use of the feminine plural ending for 'brothers' and 'fathers'.

sitt	→ sitáat	*women*
bint	→ banáat	*girls, daughters*
axx *and* uxt	→ ixwáat	*brothers, sisters*
umm	→ ummaháat	*mothers*
abb	→ abbaháat	*fathers*

Here, grouped by pattern, are the broken plurals for the singular nouns given so far.

'álam	→ a'láam	*pens*
baab	→ abwáab	*doors*
wálad	→ awláad	*boys, sons, children*
háram	→ ahráam*	*pyramids*
nahr	→ anháar	*rivers*

beet	→ buyúut	*houses*
Harb	→ Hurúub	*wars*
9een	→ 9uyúun	*eyes*
rigl	→ rugúul	*feet, legs*

*In Egypt the feminine sound plural suffix is usually added to this broken plural (= ahramáat) when referring to the ancient pyramids, while **il-ahráam** tends to be used to mean the *Al Ahram* newspaper.

madíina	→	múdun	*cities*
kitáab	→	kútub	*books*
šáari9	→	šawáari9	*streets*
gáami9	→	gawáami9	*mosques*
ginéena	→	ganáayin	*gardens*
máktab	→	makáatib	*offices, desks*
máṭ9am	→	maṭáa9im	*restaurants*
muftáaH	→	mafatíiH	*keys*
šibbáak	→	šababíik	*windows*
gurnáan	→	garaníin	*newspapers*
midáan	→	mayadíin	*city squares*
kúrsi	→	karáasi	*chairs*
kúbri	→	kabáari	*bridges*
aṛḍ	→	aṛáaḍi	*lands*
naar	→	niráan	*fires*
baHr	→	biHáar	*seas*
ṛáagil	→	riggáala	*men*
ṛaas	→	ruus	*heads*
iid	→	idéen*	*hands*

From now on the plural will be given with the singular for new vocabulary.

Subject Pronouns

	singular	plural	
ána	*I*	íHna	*we*
ínta	*you* (m.)		
ínti	*you* (f.)	íntu	*you* (pl.)
húwwa	*he, it*		
híyya	*she, it*	húmma	*they*

*__idéen__ is the dual form [cf. Lesson Four] but is used in Egypt as if it were a plural.

Simple Sentences

The structure of the Arabic equational (simple) sentence could hardly be easier. It requires only a subject and a predicate – you do *not* need the verb 'to be' in the present tense.

feen is-sawwáa'?	*Where is the driver?*
is-sawwáa' hináak	*The driver is over there.*

Additional Vocabulary

la'	*no*	min	*from*
áywa	*yes*	fi ~ f	*in*
hína	*here*	má9a ~ ma9	*with*
hináak	*there*	9ála ~ 9a	*on*
fiih	*there is*	taHt	*under*
mafíiš	*there is not*	foo'	*over*
wi ~ wa ~ w	*and*	gamb	*beside*
miš	*not*	'uddáam	*in front of*
feen?	*where?*	wáṛa	*behind*
minéen?	*from where?*	'ahwa	*coffee house*

III EXERCISES

1 Reading practice

Read the following sentences aloud, then translate them:

1. feen maHámmad?
2. húwwa fi maṣr
3. inta minéen?
4. ána min ingiltíra
5. feen ik-kitáab?
6. ik-kitáab 9ála ṭ-ṭaṛabéeza
7. il-muftáaH fil-baab?
8. la', il-muftáaH miš fil-baab
9. il-muftáaH hináak, gamb il-'álam
10. mafíiš 9arabíyya 'uddáam il-máṭ9am

2 *Translation exercise*

Translate the following:

1. feen il-wálad?
2. húwwa taHt il-kúbri.
3. il-ginéena wáṛa l-beet.
4. fiih kútub 9ála ṭ-ṭaṛabéeza?
5. áywa, fiih kútub wi 'álam 9ála ṭ-ṭaṛabéeza.
6. Where are they from?
7. They are from Egypt.
8. You (f.) are beside the window.
9. Is there a restaurant in Saad Zaghloul Square?
10. There is a restaurant there, and a coffee-house also.

LESSON TWO
(id-dars it-táani)

I COMMON EXPRESSIONS

1	áhlan wa sáhlan	*Welcome. Good to see you*
(resp.)	áhlan biik (to m.s.)	*Good to see you too*
or	áhlan bíiki (to f.s.)	
or	áhlan bíikum (to pl.)	
2	šúkran	*Thank you*
(resp.)	9áfwan	*Don't mention it*
3	má9a s-saláama	*Good-bye* (said by person staying)
(resp.)	aḷḷáah yisallímak (to m.s.)	*Good-bye* (said by person departing)
or	aḷḷáah yisallímik (to f.s.)	

or	aḷḷáah yisallímkum (to pl.)	
4	in šaa' aḷḷáah	*God-willing*

Notes

(1) The traditional expression of welcome. **ahl** is a noun meaning 'family'; **sahl**, a noun meaning 'level ground, easy to walk on', i.e. 'plain'. The accusative ending **-an**, present in both nouns, occurs only in expressions taken from CA. In the desert environment where travel was often difficult and dangerous, the original meaning was 'you have reached your family and easy ground'.
(2) The CA accusative ending **-an** is also present in **šúkran** and **9áfwan**.
(3) Lit. = 'with safety' i.e., 'go in safety' and (resp.) 'May God give you safety'.
If the person departing is the first to say goodbye, he or she may say, for example:

	sa9íida
(resp.)	ma9a s-saláama

or simply

	saláamu 9aléekum
(resp.)	9aléekum is-saláam

(4) Should be said upon any reference to the future, e.g., 'I'm travelling to Alexandria tomorrow, God-willing'. If you do not say **in šaa' aḷḷáah** in making any statement or expressing any wish or hope about the future, the Arab you are talking to will probably supply it. The underlying assumption here is that not to say it is to disregard God's control of events.

II GRAMMAR

Adjectives

An adjective may be masculine or feminine, singular or plural.

	singular		*plural*
	m.	*f.*	
big	kibíir	kibíira	kubáar
small	ṣug̲h̲ayyar	ṣug̲h̲ayyára	ṣug̲h̲ayyaríin

good	kwáyyis	kwayyísa	kwayyisíin
bad, ugly	wíHiš	wíHša	wiHšíin
beautiful	gamíil	gamíila	gumáal

(i) An adjective follows the noun it qualifies. When it qualifies a singular noun, the adjective must also be singular and agree in gender.

beet kibíir	*a big house*
madíina kibíira	*a big city*

(ii) An adjective qualifying a plural noun should also be plural when that noun refers to humans.

banáat ṣughayyaríin	*little girls*
awláad kwayyisíin	*good children*

(iii) An adjective qualifying a plural noun that refers to things (either tangible or abstract) should be feminine singular.

buyúut kibíira	*big houses*
afkáar kwayyísa	*good ideas*
lugháat sáhla	*easy languages*

(iv) An adjective qualifying a noun in its dual form must be plural regardless of whether that noun refers to humans or things. The dual will be introduced in Lesson Four.

(The student should note that rules (ii) and (iii) are not universally followed by native speakers. For example, some Egyptians use a feminine singular adjective to qualify even certain 'human' nouns, e.g. **il-banáat iṣ-ṣughayyára**; and some use the plural form of the adjective to qualify nouns referring to things, particularly tangible objects, e.g. **il-buyúut il-kubáar**. Nevertheless, the student will find it easier in the long run always to use (i) a plural adjective to refer to humans in the plural; and (ii) a feminine singular adjective to qualify all non-'human' plural nouns.)

If the noun is definite (i.e. preceded by the definite article), the adjective must also be definite.

il-beet il-kibíir	*the big house*
il-madíina l-kibíira	*the big city*
il-awláad ik-kwayyisíin	*the good children*

If the adjective is left indefinite, an adjectival phrase is turned into an equational sentence.

il-beet kibíir	*The house is big*

Learn the following adjectives in pairs:

	singular		*plural*
	m.	*f.*	
new	gidíid	gidíida	gudáad
*old**	'adíim	'adíima	'udáam
tall, long	ṭawíil	ṭawíila	ṭuwáal
short	'uṣáyyar	'uṣayyára	'uṣayyaríin
expensive	g͟háali	g͟hálya	g͟halyíin
cheap	rixíiṣ	rixíiṣa	ruxáaṣ
clean	niḍíif	niḍíifa	nuḍáaf
*dirty***	wísix	wísxa	awsáax
lightweight	xafíif	xafíifa	xufáaf
heavy	ti'íil	ti'íila	tu'áal
near	'uráyyib	'urayyíba	'urayyibíin
far	bi9íid	bi9íida	bu9áad
easy	sahl	sáhla	sahlíin
difficult	ṣa9b	ṣá9ba	ṣa9bíin
generous	karíim	karíima	kúrama
miser(ly)	baxíil	baxíila	búxala
thin	rufáyya9	rufayyá9a	rufayya9íin
fat	tixíin	tixíina	tuxáan

*When referring to an 'old' person, Arabs use **kibíir** or the phrase **kibíir fis-sinn** (= 'big in age'). Similarly 'young' is **ṣaghíir** or **ṣaghíir fis-sinn**.
Egyptians ofter prefer to say **miš naḍíif (= 'not clean'), leaving **wísix** to mean filthy or 'morally dirty'.

The following adjectives are of two common patterns not represented above. They take **-a** in the feminine and, with one exception, the masculine sound plural. When adding the **-iin** for the plural remember to shorten the preceding long vowel.

kasláan	*lazy*
ta9báan	*tired*
9ayyáan	*sick*
za9láan	*angry*
xarbáan	*broken (down)*
magnúun (pl. maganíin)	*crazy*
mabsúuṭ	*happy*
mašghúul	*busy*

Nisba adjectives

Another type of adjective is that formed by adding **--i** to the related noun. We do something similar in English when from 'oil' we derive the adjective 'oily', or from 'Iraq' its adjective 'Iraqi'. In Arabic these are called 'Nisba' adjectives. The adjectives below are all Nisba-type, though the original noun may be slightly modified to form the stem for the adjectival endings. Note also that not all the plurals are of the masculine sound type.*

Place names		*Adjectives*		
		m.	*f.*	*pl.*
Egypt	maṣr	máṣri	maṣríyya	maṣriyyíin
Syria	súrya	súuri	suríyya	suriyyíin
Lebanon	libnáan	libnáani	libnaníyya	libnaniyyíin
Iraq	il-9iráa'	9iráa'i	9ira'íyya	9ira'iyyíin
England	ingiltíra	ingilíizi	ingiliziyya	ingilíiz

*Don't be surprised to hear any or all of the following from native speakers:

il-banáat il-maṣríyya
il-banáat il-maṣriyyíin
il-banáat il-maṣriyyáat

The last, where the adjective has a feminine sound plural ending, is a direct borrowing from CA.

America	amríika	amrikáani	amrikaníyya	amrikáan
the East	iš-šar'	šár'i	šar'íyya	šar'iyyíin
the West	il-gharb	ghárbi	gharbíyya	gharbiyyíin

Also important in the context of Nisba adjectives are the words for 'Arab(ic)': **9árabi** (m.s.), **9arabíyya** (f.s.) and **9árab** (pl.)

inglíizi and **9árabi** also mean the languages English and Arabic.

bil-ingilíizi	*in English*
bil-9árabi	*in Arabic*

Note that any adjective can be used as a noun.

ig-gidíid	*the new [one]*
il-maṣríyya	*the Egyptian woman*
il-inglíiz	*the English*

Additional vocabulary

kílma (kilmáat)	*word*	'áwi	*very*
gúmla (gúmal)	*sentence*	gíddan	*very*
lúgha (lugháat)	*language*	xáaliṣ	*extremely*
ziyáara (ziyaráat)	*visit*	wálla	*or*
láakin	*but*	la . . . wála	*neither . . . nor*
innahárda	*today*	ya	vocative partical, used before a name when addressing someone directly
xaddáam (xaddamíin)	*servant*		
miš mawgund = miš hina	*not present*		

III EXERCISES

1 Reading practice: a dialogue

ziyáara 'uṣayyára 'áwi

A. áhlan wa sáhlan, ya samíira!
B. áhlan biik, ya maHmúud.

A. izzáyyik innahárda?
B. kwayyísa, l-Hámdu lilláah. w-ínta?
A. kwáyyis, il-Hámdu lilláah.
B. nágwa miš hína?
A. la, híyya f-iskindiríyya nnahárda.
B. šúkran. sa9íida.
A. má9a s-saláama.

2 *Translation exercise*

1. il-maṣriyyíin kúrama.
2. in-niil nahr gamíil wi ṭawíil xáaliṣ!
3. il-ahramáat bi9íida min hína?
4. ínta súuri wálla libnáani?
5. ána la súuri wála libnáani. ána máṣri.
6. The word is easy.
7. In Egypt restaurants [= the restaurants] are inexpensive.
8. War [= the war] is bad.
9. The sentence is not difficult.
10. The table is dirty [= not clean], but the servant is not here.

LESSON THREE
(id-dars it-táalit)

I COMMON EXPRESSIONS

1		misáa' il-xeer	*Good evening*
	(resp.)	misáa' in-nuur	*Good evening*
2		itfáḍḍal (to m.s.)	*Please, go ahead*
	or	itfaḍḍáli (to f.s.)	
	or	itfaḍḍálu (to pl.)	
	(resp.)	šúkran	*Thank you*
3		fúrṣa sa9íida	*Pleased to meet you*
	(resp.)	íHna ás9ad	*My pleasure*

4 sallímli 9ála – (to m.s.) *Remember me to –*
or sallimíili 9ála – (to f.s.)
or sallimúuli 9ála – (to pl.)

Notes

(1) Lit. = 'evening of goodness' and (resp.) 'evening of light'. There are no variations to the response.
(2) A more literal translation would be 'be so kind'. It may be used to mean 'after you' (at the door); or 'please be seated'; or 'please take some' (of whatever is being offered).
(3) Lit. = 'happy occasion' and (resp.) 'we are happier'. The response is always in the first person plural ('we') even when the person responding is speaking for him or her self alone.
(4) Or 'give my regards to –'. Arabs everywhere know the line sung by Egyptian singer **9abd ul-Halíim Háafiz**: **w-in la'áakum Habíibi, sallimúuli 9aléeh** ('if my love should meet you, give her my regards').

II GRAMMAR

Construct Phrases

The term 'construct phrase' denotes two words juxtaposed in what may be considered a direct 'possessed-possessor' relationship. Only the second noun can carry the definite article even though both may be definite. In English this relationship could be indicated by putting the word 'of' between the two nouns, as in 'the book of the girl' (i.e., 'the girl's book'). In Arabic this would be

kitáab il-bint

When the first noun in a construct phrase is feminine and ends in **-a** (e.g. **9arabíyya**), the **-a** changes to **-it**.

9arabíyyit is-sitt *the woman's car*

Proper nouns (e.g. names of people or places) are definite without needing the definite article. Note, however, that the definite article is retained if it forms part of the name, as in **il-qaahíra**.

kitáab maHámmad	*Muhammad's book*
medíinit aswáan	*the city of Aswan*
medíinit il-qaahíra	*the city of Cairo*

To say 'the book of a girl' (i.e. 'a girl's book') one drops the definite article from the second noun.

kitáab bint

Adjectives modifying either noun must follow the construct phrase.

baab il-beet il-kibíir	*the big door of the house* or *the door of the big house*

If the meaning is not clear from the context, ambiguity can be avoided by using the alternative to the construct phrase described in the following section.

'bitáa9'

A common alternative to the construct phrase is the use of the word **bitáa9** (of) (fem. = **bitáa9it** or **bitá9t**, pl. = **bitúu9**).

il-kitáab bitáa9 il-bint	*the girl's book*
il-9arabíyya bitáa9it is-sitt	*the woman's car*
il-baab il-kibíir bitáa9 il-beet	*the big door of the house*
il-baab bitáa9 il-beet il-kibíir	*the door of the big house*
il-awláad bitúu9 il-falláaH	*the farmer's children*

Pronominal suffixes

Pronominal suffixes may be attached to nouns, prepositions, and verbs. In translation the suffixes appear as possessive pronouns, objects of prepositions, or direct objects. They differ slightly depending on whether the words to which they are added end in a consonant or a vowel (but *not* the feminine **--a**).

after consonants

--i	béeti	*my house*
--ak	béetak	*your* (m.) *house*
--ik	béetik	*your* (f.) *house*
--uh	béetuh	*his house*

--ha	bétha*	*her house*
--na	bétna*	*our house*
--kum	bétkum*	*your* (pl.) *house*
--hum	béthum*	*their house*

after vowels

--ya	ma9áaya	*with me* or *I have*
--k	ma9áak	*with you* (m.) or *you have*
--ki	ma9áaki	*with you* (f.) or *you have*
--h	ma9áah	*with him* or *he has*
--ha	ma9áaha	*with her* or *she has*
--na	ma9áana	*with us* or *we have*
--kum	ma9áakum	*with you* (pl.) or *you have*
--hum	ma9áahum	*with them* or *they have*

Note the lengthening of the final vowel of the base word. This lengthening occurs in all base words ending in a vowel to which a suffix is added.

A common alternative to the 2nd pers. pl. suffix **--kum** is **--ku**.

Feminine nouns ending in **--a** take their 'construct form' (i.e. end in **--it**) before the pronominal suffixes.

9arabiyyítha	*her automobile*

The various forms of **bitáa9** may also be used in combination with the pronominal suffixes.

il-beet bitá9na	*our house*
il-9arabíyya bitá9ti	*my car*
il-awláad bitú9ha	*her children*

'To have'

A combination of the preposition **9and** and one of the pronominal suffixes is the usual way of saying 'to have'.

9ándi	*I have*	9andína**	*we have*
9ándak	*you* (m.s.) *have*	9andúkum**	*you* (pl.) *have*

*Egyptian Arabic does not allow VVCC.

**Notice the extra vowel added to prevent a three-consonant cluster.

9ándik	*you* (f.s.) *have*	9andúhum**	*they have*
9ánduh	*he, it has*		
9andáha**	*she, it has*		

The *negative forms are*:

ma9andíiš	ma9andináaš
ma9andákš	ma9andukúmš
ma9andikíiš	ma9anduhúmš
ma9andúuš	
ma9anduháaš	

Examples:

9ándak filúus?	*Do you have [any] money?*
ma9andíiš Háaga	*I don't have anything.*

Demonstratives

(i)

da (m.s.)	*this/that*
di (f.s.)	*this/that*
dool (pl.)	*these/those*

These words may occur after the noun (as demonstrative adjectives) or before the noun (as demonstrative pronouns).
Examples:

da kitáab kwáyyis	*This (or that) is a good book.*
il-kitáab da kwáyyis	*This (or that) book is good.*
di bint maṣríyya	*That is an Egyptian girl.*
il-bint di maṣríyya	*That girl is Egyptian.*
dool sawwa'íin wiHšíin	*Those are bad drivers.*
is-sawwa'íin dool wiHšíin	*Those drivers are bad.*

(ii)
Usually classified with the demonstratives are:

ahó (m.s.)	*here is/there is*
ahé (f.s.)	*here is/there is*
ahúm (pl.)	*here are/there are*

These words may precede or follow the noun, or occur in isolation. Examples:

feen il-lukánḍa?	*Where is the hotel?*
ahé l-lukánḍa	*There is the hotel.*
il-lukánḍa hé	
ahé!	*There it is!*
feen ig-gurnáan?	*Where is the newspaper?*
ahó!	*There it is!*
il-fallaHíin feen?	*Where are the peasants?*
ahúm!	*There they are!*

IMPORTANT TO REMEMBER: Non-human plural nouns, both tangible and abstract, should, unless dual (explained in Lesson Four), always be treated syntactically as if they were feminine singular.

il-buyúut *di kibíira*	*Those houses are big.*
il-9arabiyyáat *bitáa9it* iš-šírka feen?	*Where are the company's cars?*
il-9arabiyyáat *ahé!*	*There are the cars!*

Additional vocabulary

ism (asáami)	*name*
Háaga (Hagáat)	*thing*
filúus (f.)	*money*
lukánḍa (lukanḍáat)	*hotel*
fúndu' (fanáadi')	*hotel* (Classical Arabic)
utéel	*hotel*
šírka (širkáat)	*company*
šánṭa (šúnaṭ)	*suitcase, briefcase, lady's bag*
borg (burúug)	*tower*
gám9a (gam9áat)	*university*
gumhuríyya (gumhuriyyáat)	*republic*
bawwáab (bawwabíin)	*doorman*
mudíir (mudiríin)	*director, manager*
ra'íis (rú'asa)	*president, chief*
misáafir (misafríin)	*traveller*
ṭayyáara (ṭayyaráat)	*airplane*

maṭáar (maṭaráat)	*airport*
borg il-qaahíra	*Cairo Tower*
midáan it-taHríir	*Liberation Square*
maṣr ig-gidíida	*Heliopolis* (a Cairo suburb)
'uráyyib min	*near* (s.th.)
bi9íid 9an	*far from* (s.th.)
bass	*only, just; but*
eeh?	*what?*

III EXERCISES

1 Reading practice

ísmak eeh?
ísmi David Smith.
béetak feen?
béeti 'uráyyib min borg il-qaahíra.

feen il-muftáaH bitáa9 baab il-máktab?
muftáaH il-baab da má9a l-bawwáab.

il-9arabíyya di bitáa9it miin?
híyya bitáa9it ra'íis il-gumhuríyya.

gám9it il-qaahíra fig-gíiza wig-gám9a l-amrikaníyya fi midáan it-taHríir.

iš-šánta di gidíida.
šántit il-misáafir gidíida.
šántit il-misáafir il-9ayyáan fiṭ-ṭayyáara.

2 Translation exercise

1. ísmuh eeh?
2. beet il-mudíir fi maṣr ig-gidíida
3. il-fallaHíin dool ta9baníin innahárda
4. ána 9ándi kitáab wi 'álam, láakin hiyya ma9andaháaš la kitáab wála 'álam
5. il-9arabíyya bitá9tak ahé bass il-9arabíyya bitá9ti feen?
6. Where is your (pl.) house?
7. We don't have a house.

8. That university is extremely expensive.
9. There is the hotel, but where is the restaurant?
10. The director's new suitcase is at the airport.

LESSON FOUR
(id-dars ir-ráabi9)

I COMMON EXPRESSIONS

1	min fáḍlak (to m.s.) or min fáḍlik (to f.s.) or min faḍlúkum (to pl.)	*Please*
2	áasif (to m.s.) or ásfa (to f.s.) or asfíin (to pl.)	*Sorry*
(resp.)	ma9líšš	*It doesn't matter; never mind*
3	yálla	*Let's go*

Notes

(1) Lit. = 'from your kindness'. If someone uses this expression when asking for something (e.g. at the table), the response, when handing the thing over, would be **itfaḍḍal**. You will also hear the response **Háaḍir**, particularly from waiters, meaning 'at your service'. This is invariably masculine.
(2) Also **mit'ássif** (m.), **mit'assífa** (f.), and **mit'assifíin** (pl.). Note that **ma9líšš** is one of the commonest expressions in Colloquial Arabic, used when something petty goes wrong or when someone does not get his or her way.
(3) Originally an invocation **ya alláah** (O God), the connotation has changed to mean 'let's go'; also said in the form of **yálla bíina**. **yálla** by itself may also mean 'hurry up!'

II GRAMMAR

Numbers (il-a9dáad)

Cardinals 1–100

1	wáaHid, wáHda	20	9išríin
2	itnéen	21	wáaHid wi-9išríin
3	taláata	22	itnéen wi-9išríin
4	árba9a	23	taláata w-9išríin
5	xámsa	24	árba9a w-9išríin
6	sítta	25	xámsa w-9išríin
7	sáb9a	26	sítta w-9išríin
8	tamánya	27	sáb9a w-9išríin
9	tís9a	28	tamánya w-9išríin
10	9ášara	29	tís9a w-9išríin
11	Hidáašar	30	talatíin
12	itnáašar	31	wáaHid wi-talatíin etc.
13	talaṭṭáašar	40	arbi9íin
14	arba9ṭáašar	50	xamsíin
15	xamasṭáašar	60	siṭṭíin
16	siṭṭáašar	70	sab9íin
17	saba9ṭáašar	80	tamaníin
18	tamanṭáašar	90	tis9íin
19	tisa9ṭáašar	100	míyya

Number 'one' is the only number which has two forms to show gender. It is also the only number that generally follows the noun.

9aṣkári wáaHid	*one policeman*
sitt wáHda	*one lady*

It may, however, precede a noun referring to humans in which case the meaning changes.

wáaHid 9askári	*a policeman*, or *some policeman* ('*I don't know who*')
wáHda sitt	*a woman, some woman or other*

To indicate 'two' of something Arabic usually uses the dual form of the noun without use of the numeral. The dual consists of the noun plus the suffix **--een**. Feminine singular nouns ending in **--a** take their construct form (**--it**) before the suffix.

waladéen	*two boys*
betéen	*two houses*
oḍtéen [for oḍiteen]	*two rooms*

Nouns ending in a vowel (other than the feminine ending **--a**), take a 'y' between that vowel and the dual suffix.

kursiyéen	*two chairs*

There are rare exceptions where the dual is generally not used with a particular noun. For example, with the word **sitt** the numeral 'two' is used before the plural form of the noun.

itnéen sittáat	*two women*

As noted in Lesson Two an adjective qualifying any noun in the dual form must be plural.

kursiyéen kubáar	*two big chairs*

For the numbers 'three' to 'ten' Egyptian Arabic has a 'short form' used before nouns, which must be plural.

3	tálat	7	sába9
4	árba9	8	táman
5	xámas	9	tísa9
6	sitt	10	9ášar

Examples:

tálat banáat	*3 girls*
9ášar maṛṛáat	*10 times*

A few counted nouns, including those denoting drinks ordered (in a restaurant, for example) are always in the singular, while the numbers stay in their regular 'long form'.

itnéen ginéeh	*2 pounds*
taláata 'áhwa, min fáḍlak	*3 coffees, please*
árba9a kíilu mooz	*4 kilograms of bananas*

From number ‘eleven’ on the counted noun must be in the singular form.

Hidáašar máṛṛa	*11 times*
tís9a w-talatíin ’irš	*39 piasters*
wáaHid wi-xamsíin kitáab	*51 books*

Although the usual word for ‘hundred’ is **miyya**, ‘100 of something’ is expressed using **miit** before the counted noun instead. Note that this only applies to ‘100 . . .’, not to ‘101/102/110 *etc* . . .’.

miit yoom	*100 days*
míyya w-xamsíin yoom	*150 days*

Beyond ‘199’:

200	*mitéen*
300	*tultumíyya*
400	*rub9umíyya*
500	*xumsumíyya*
600	*suttumíyya*
700	*sub9umíyya*
800	*tumnumíyya*
900	*tus9umíyya*
1,000	*alf*
1,000,000	*milyóon*
1,000,000,000	*bilyóon*

Examples:

mitéen wi-9ášara sána	*210 years*
tultumíit ṛáagil	*300 men*
xumsumíyya tís9a w-tis9íin duláar	*$599*
alf tus9umíyya sítta w-xamsíin	*1956*
xámsa milyóon 9áṛabi	*5,000,000 Arabs*
bilyóon barmíil zeet	*1,000,000,000 barrels of oil*

Ordinals

m.	*f.*	
áwwil	úula	*first*
táani	tánya	*second*

táalit	tálta	*third*
ṛáabi9	ráb9a	*fourth*
xáamis	xámsa	*fifth*
sáadis	sádsa	*sixth*
sáabi9	sáb9a	*seventh*
táamin	támna	*eighth*
táasi9	tás9a	*ninth*
9áašir	9ášra	*tenth*

To form ordinals for numbers higher than 'ten' just prefix **il-** to the cardinal form of the number.

il-Hidáašar	*eleventh*
il-arbá9a w-talatíin	*34th*

Learn also:

m.	f.	
awwaláani	awwalaníyya	*The first* [one], *the former*
wasṭáani	wasṭaníyya	*middle* (adj.); *average*
axíir	axíira	*last*
axṛáani	axṛaníyya	*the other* [one]; *the latter*

áaxir also means 'last', but it must occur before the noun.

iṛ-ṛáagil il-wasṭáani	*the man in the middle*
il-kílma l-axíira	*the last word*
áaxir wáaHid	*the last one* (note that in the Arabic the article is implicit but not expressed)

Easy fractions

nuṣṣ	*1/2*
tilt	*1/3*
rub9	*1/4*
xums	*1/5*
suds	*1/6*
sub9	*1/7*
tumn	*1/8*
tus9	*1/9*

9ušr	*1/10*
tiltéen	*2/3*
xụmséen	*2/5*
talat arbaa9	*3/4*

Telling the time

is-sáa9a kaam min fáḍlak?	*What time is it, please?*
is-sáa9a wáHda	*It's 1:00.*
is-sáa9a wáHda w-xámsa	*It's 1:05.*
is-sáa9a wáHda w-9ášara	*It's 1:10.*
is-sáa9a wáHda w-rub9	*It's 1:15.*
is-sáa9a wáHda w-tilt	*It's 1:20.*
is-sáa9a wáHda w-nuṣṣ ílla xámsa	*It's 1:25.*
is-sáa9a wáHda w-nuṣṣ	*It's 1:30.*
is-sáa9a wáHda w-nuṣṣ wi xámsa	*It's 1:35.*
is-sáa9a tnéen ílla tilt	*It's 1:40.*
is-sáa9a tnéen ílla rub9	*It's 1:45.*
is-sáa9a tnéen ílla 9ášara	*It's 1:50.*
is-sáa9a tnéen ílla xámsa	*It's 1:55.*
is-sáa9a tnéen biẓ-ẓabṭ	*It's 2:00 exactly.*
is-sáa9a taláata	*It's 3:00.*

etc.

Months (iš-šuhuur)

yanáayir	*January*
fibráayir	*February*
máaris	*March*
abríil	*April*
máayu	*May*
yúnyu	*June*
yúlyu	*July*
ag͟húsṭus	*August*
sebtémber	*September*
uktúubar	*October*

nuvámbir	*November*
disímbir	*December*

Islamic months

muHárram
ṣáfar
rabíi9 il-áwwal
rabíi9 it-táani
gamáad il-áwwal
gamáad it-táani
rágab
ša9báan
ramaḍáan
šawáal
zu-l-qí9da
zu-l-Hígga

The 12 islamic months are lunar, and so do not correlate at all to the western calendar. The lunar 'year' is eleven days shorter than ours, so the months move forward every year.

Days of the week (ayyáam il-usbúu9)

yoom il-itnéen	*Monday*
yoom it-taláat	*Tuesday*
yoom il-árba9	*Wednesday*
yoom il-xamíis	*Thursday*
yoom il-gúm9a	*Friday*
yoom is-sabt	*Saturday*
yoom il-Hadd	*Sunday*

Seasons (il-fuṣúul)

iṣ-ṣeef	*summer*
il-xaríif	*autumn, fall*
iš-šíta	*winter*
ir-rabíi9	*spring*

More time expressions

innahárda	*today*
búkra	*tomorrow*
imbáariH	*yesterday*
ba9d búkra	*the day after tomorrow*
áwwil imbáariH	*the day before yesterday*
dilwá'ti	*now*
ba9d šwáyya	*in a little while*
iṣ-ṣubH	*(in) the morning*
iḍ-ḍuhr	*(at) noon*
ba9d iḍ-ḍuhr	*afternoon*
il-9aṣr	*mid-afternoon*
misáa'an	*in the evening*
bil-leel	*at night*
nuṣṣ il-leel	*midnight*

Additional Vocabulary

9askári (9asáakir)	*policeman; soldier*
mutárgim (mutargimíin)	*translator*
óḍa (owaḍ)	*room*
máṛṛa (maṛṛáat)	*time* (as in 'two times'); *once*
'irš ('urúuš)	*piaster*
ginéeh	*pound* (Egyptian or Sterling)
'áhwa	*coffee*
šaay	*tea*
mooz	*bananas* (collective)
sáa9a (sa9áat)	*hour; watch, clock*
di'íi'a (da'áayi')	*minute*
sánya (sawáani)	*second*
yoom (ayyáam)	*day*
usbúu9 (asabíi9)	*week*
šahr (ášhur or šuhúur)	*month*
sána (siníin)	*year*
9adad (a9dáad)	*number*
nímra (nímar)	*number*
faṣl (fuṣúul)	*season*
barmíil (baramíil)	*barrel*

zeet (zuyúut)	*oil*
dars (durúus)	*lesson*
bálad (f.) (biláad)	*country*
tazkára (tazáakir)	*ticket*
nuṣṣ	*half*
rub9	*quarter*
tilt	*third*
ílla	*minus; except*
biẓ-ẓabṭ	*precisely*
bass	*only*
li	*for*
lágna (ligáan)	*commission*

III EXERCISES

1 Reading practice

alf tus9umíyya xámsa w-tamaníin.
ma9áana mutargiméen kwayyisíin innahárda, l-awwaláani min bag͟hdáad wil-axṛáani min dimíš'.
wáaHid 'áhwa w-itnéen šaay min fáḍlak.
is-sáa9a sítta w-nuṣṣ ílla xámsa iṣ-ṣubH.
9ášara 'urúuš.
xámsa w-xamsíin 'irš.
xámsa ginéeh máṣri.
xamasṭáašar ginéeh sterlíini.
fis-sána tnáašar šahr.
lug͟hitéen ṣa9bíin.

2 Translation exercise

1. il-xámas kútub di g͟hálya.
2. léela 9andáha tnéen wi-9išríin sána.
3. 9ánduh dars ba9d iḍ-ḍuhr yoom il-itnéen.
4. fiih Háfla s-sáa9a sáb9a w-nuṣṣ misáa'an.
5. ma9andináaš mitéen duláar lit-tazáakir.
6. Where are those five ladies?
7. There are twenty servants in that villa.
8. The eleventh man is not here.

9. Lebanon is a small country, but it has [*lit*: in it are] six million [sítta milyóon] Lebanese.
10. Those two big cars belong to the president of the Commission.

LESSON FIVE
(id-dars il-xáamis)

I COMMON EXPRESSIONS

1		tíṣbaH 9ála xeer (to m.s.)	*Good night*
	or	tiṣbáHi 9ála xeer (to f.s.)	
	or	tiṣbáHu 9ála xeer (to pl.)	
	(resp.)	w-ínta min áhluh (to m.s.)	*Good night*
	or	w-ínti min áhluh (to f.s.)	
	or	w-íntu min áhluh (to pl.)	
2		mabrúuk	*Congratulations*
	(resp.)	aḷḷáah yibáarik fiik (to m.s.)	*Thank you*
	or	aḷḷáah yibáarik fíiki (to f.s.)	
	or	aḷḷáah yibáarik fíikum (to pl.)	
3		ríHla sa9íida	*Have a good trip*
4		Hamdílla 9as-saláama	*Welcome back*
	(resp.)	Aḷḷáah yisallímak, etc.	

Notes

(1) Lit. = 'may you wake up in the morning to [lit. on] goodness' and (resp.) 'and you are one of [lit: from] its people' (i.e. people of goodness).
(2) Lit. = 'blessed' and (resp.) 'God gives blessing in you'.
(3) Lit. = 'happy trip'.
(4) A condensed form of **il-Hámdu lilláah 9ála s-saláama**. Lit. = 'praise [be] to God for [your] safety.'

II GRAMMAR

Interrogative words

eeh?	*what?*
feen?	*where?*
izzáay?	*how?*
miin?	*who?*
ímta?	*when?*
leeh?	*why?*
kaam?	*how many?*
'add eeh?	*how much?*

izzaay changes to **izzayy** before suffixes.

izzáyyak?	*How are you?*

When **kaam** immediately precedes a noun, that noun must be singular.

9ándak kaam wálad?	*How many children do you have?*

Interrogative words often come at the end of a sentence.

ismáha eeh?	*What's her name?*
is-sáa9a kaam?	*What time is it?*

Active Participles

Active participles are like adjectives in that they are inflected for gender and number, but they have verbal meaning. They may stand alone or in equational sentences.

	m.	*f.*	*pl.*
want(ing)	9áawiz	9áwza	9awzíin
	9áayiz	9áyza	9ayzíin
know(ing)	9áarif	9árfa	9arfíin
understand(ing)	fáahim	fáhma	fahmíin
go(ing)	ráayiH	ráyHa	rayHíin
do(ing)	9áamil	9ámla	9amlíin

stay(ing) or *sit(ting)*	'áa9id	'á9da	'a9díin
stop(ing) or *stand(ing)*	wáa'if	wá'fa	wa'fíin
see(ing)	šáayif	šáyfa	šayfíin
*live (living)**	sáakin	sákna	sakníin
sleep(ing)	náayim	náyma	naymíin
come (coming)	gaay	gáyya	gayyíin

Examples:

	fáahim	*I understand* *You* (m.s.) *understand* *He understands*
	fáhma	*You* (f.s.) *understand* *She understands*
	fahmíin	*We understand* *You* (pl.) *understand* *They understand*
(interrogative)	fáahim?	*Do you understand?* etc.
(negative)	miš fáahim	*I do not understand* etc.
(negative-interrogative)	miš fáahim?	*Don't you understand?* etc.

Adverbial phrases with 'bi-'

A common way to form adverbs is to prefix **bi--** ('with' or 'by') to the appropriate noun.

bi-ṣu9úuba *with difficulty*
bi-suhúula *easily*

*in the sense of 'residing'.

bi-súr9a	*quickly*
bi-šwees	*slowly*

(The last expression naturally falls with the others although there is no noun **šwees** existing independently.)

Learn also the following adverbial phrases:

biṭ-ṭayyáara	*by plane*
bil-9arabíyya	*by automobile*
bil-9ágala	*by bicycle*
bil-'aṭr	*by train*
bil-utubíis	*by bus*

Additional vocabulary

suhúula	*ease*
ṣu9úuba	*difficulty*
9ágala (9agaláat)	*bicycle*
'aṭr ('uṭuṛáat)	*train*
utubíis (utubisáat)	*bus*
šá''a (šú'a')	*apartment*
safíir (súfara)	*ambassador*
sifáara (sifaráat)	*embassy*
gooz (agwáaz)	*husband*
miṛáatu*	*his wife*
lig͟háayit	*until*
kull Háaga	*everything*

III EXERCISES

1 Reading practice

ráayiH feen?
ráayiH is-sifáara l-biriṭaníyya.

il-awláad 9amlíin eeh dilwá'ti?
naymíin.

*The original word is **mára** ('woman'), which is somewhat vulgar in Egyptian Arabic unless used with a pronominal suffix or in construct, e.g. **miṛáati** ('my wife') and **miṛáat 9áli** ('Ali's wife').

9áli sáakin fid-dó''i.
w-ínti sákna feen?
ána w-góozi sakníin fi šá''a gidíida fi šáari9 Hásan ṣábri.

miin gaay min il-maṭáar innahárda?
waḷḷáahi, miš 9árfa.

iš-šírka di 9áyza kaam 9arabíyya gidíida?
9áyza miteen.
miš ma9'úul!

2 Translation exercise

1. ínta ráayiH izzáay? biṭ-ṭayyáara?
2. 9awzíin 'add eeh?
3. ána miš 9áarif nímrit it-tilifúun bitáa9it is-safíir.
4. miṛáatuh wá'fa fiš-šáaṛi9 wi-9arabiyyítha xarbáana.
5. muṣṭáfa 'áa9id 9andína lig͟háayit yoom il-xamíis.
6. They are coming by bus.
7. My wife wants three kilos of bananas.
8. Does Mustapha live in Doqqi or in Giza?
9. Do you understand everything?
10. Is the bus coming quickly or slowly?

LESSON SIX
(id-dars is-sáadis)

I COMMON EXPRESSIONS

1		la mu'áxsa	*Excuse me*
	(resp.)	ma9líšš	*It's nothing*
2		ismáHli (to m.s.)	*Excuse me*
	or	ismaHíili (to f.s.)	
	or	ismaHúuli (to pl.)	
	(resp.)	itfáḍḍal etc.	

3		9an íznak (to m.s.)	*Excuse me*
	or	9an íznik (to f.s.)	
	or	9an iznúkum (to pl.)	
(resp.)		itfáḍḍal etc.	

Notes

(1) Lit. = 'no resentment [I hope]', i.e. 'I hope you have not taken offence.' Used, for example, by someone who is the cause of a minor accident such as stepping on someone else's foot or spilling something on or near some person.
(2) Lit. = 'permit me' and used, e.g. if someone is blocking the speaker's way, or if the speaker wants to politely interrupt someone.
(3) Lit. = 'with your permission'. Can be used like **ismáHli** but has the additional meaning of 'Excuse me. I have to leave now.' This latter meaning may also be conveyed by the verbal form **astá'zin**.

II GRAMMAR

Comparative and superlative adjectives

The comparative (and superlative) form of the adjective is invariable, i.e. not inflected for gender and number. For most of the adjectives given so far, the pattern for the comparative is **aCCaC**.

kibíir	ákbar	*bigger*
ṣug͟háyyar	áṣg͟har	*smaller*
gamíil	ágmal	*more beautiful*

When the second and third root letters of the adjective are identical (e.g. **xafíif**), the comparative pattern is usually **aCaCC**, but occasionally **aCCaC**.

xafíif	axáff	*lighter (in weight)*
gidíid	ágdad	*newer*

Adjectives ending in **-w** or **-i** form the comparative according to the pattern **aCCa**.

Hilw	áHla	*sweeter, prettier*
gháali	ághla	*more expensive*

The comparative of **kwáyyis** ('good') is **áHsan** ('better'). The word for 'than' in Arabic comparative structures is **min**.

ana ákbar mínnak *I'm bigger than you*

Colours (il-alwáan)

	m.	*f.*	*pl.*
red	áHmar	Hámra	Humr
green	áxḍar	xáḍra	xuḍr
blue	ázra'	zár'a	zur'
yellow	áṣfar	ṣáfra	ṣufr
white	ábyaḍ	béeḍa	biiḍ
black	íswid	sóoda	suud
brown	búnni	búnni	búnni
grey	ramáadi	ramáadi	ramáadi
orange	burtu'áani	burtu'áani	burtu'áani

Of the same basic pattern (**aCCaC**) are adjectives denoting certain physical disabilities.

blind	á9ma	9ámya	9umy
deaf	áṭraš	ṭárša	ṭurš
dumb, mute	áxras	xársa	xurs
lame	á9rag	9árga	9urg
one-eyed	á9war	9óora	9uur

It is worth noting that an Egyptian would probably say 'he cannot see' rather than 'he is blind'; 'he has one eye' rather than 'he is one-eyed', etc. There is a definite preference for using what is considered a polite circumlocution to direct mention of an adjective of physical disability. On the other hand, **á9war** might be considered an appropriate insult for a bad driver!

III EXERCISES

1 Reading practice

ána ákbar mínnak bi-tálat siníin.
il-ba'láawa áHsan min iž-žiláati.

miin sáakin fil-beet il-ábyaḍ da?
muníira gamíila, láakin faríida ágmal.
il-9arabíyya l-Hámra ágdad min il-9arabíyya l-xáḍra.
eeh il-ashal, 9árabi wálla ingilíizi?
il-oḍtéen dool ṣug̲h̲ayyaríin 'áwi!

2 Translation exercise

1. Hásan áṣg̲h̲ar min ráamiz.
2. is-sáwwaa' da á9war. húwwa sawwáa' wíHiš.
3. ir-rabíi9 áHla l-fuṣúul.
4. it-tuffáaH kwáyyis láakin il-burtu'áan áHsan.
5. il-kitabéen dool ruxáaṣ.
6. I am lighter (in weight) than Hassan.
7. Summer is nicer than winter.
8. Those two girls are beautiful, but his sister is more beautiful.
9. Alexandria is one of the [from the] most beautiful Egyptian cities.
10. How much for those two blue pens.

LESSON SEVEN (id-dars is-sáabi9)

I COMMON EXPRESSIONS

1		wala yhímmak (to m.s.)	*Don't worry!*
	or	wala yhímmik (to f.s.)	
	or	wala yhimmúkum (to pl.)	
2		xálli báalak (to m.s.)	*Be careful*
	or	xálli báalik (to f.s.)	
	or	xállu bálkum (to pl.)	
3		Háasib (to m.s.)	*Look out!*
	or	Hásbi (to f.s.)	
	or	Hásbu (to pl.)	
4		ya xsáara	*What a pity!*

Notes

(1) Lit. = '[and] let it not worry you.'
(2) Also 'pay attention'. Takes the prepositions **min** or **9ála**.
(3) May convey a sense of urgency or imminent danger (e.g. a fast approaching car, something about to fall, etc.).
(4) **xasáara** = loss. The particle **ya** introduces vocative expressions. Lit. = 'O loss!'

II GRAMMAR

Perfect Tense (Simple Verbs)

There are two basic tenses in Arabic. The 'perfect', denoting action which is finished, corresponds to the English past tense. The 'imperfect' refers to action which is incomplete (either on-going or future) and corresponds to our present, progressive and future tenses.

There is no infinitive form of the verb in Arabic. A verb is referred to by the 3rd person masculine singular of its perfect tense. This is also how the verb appears in a dictionary.

The simple verb **kátab** 'he wrote' is conjugated in the perfect tense as follows:

(ána) katábt	*I wrote*
(ínta) katábt	*you* (m.s.) *wrote*
(ínti) katábti	*you* (f.s.) *wrote*
(húwwa) kátab	*he wrote*
(híyya) kátabit	*she wrote*
(íHna) katábna	*we wrote*
(íntu) katábtu	*you* (pl.) *wrote*
(húmma) kátabu	*they wrote*

Taking **kátab** as the shortest and simplest form in this conjugation, one finds that the other persons are indicated by the addition of suffixes. Where the suffix causes a cluster of two consonants there is also a change in stress.

The shape of the simple verb is not always **CaCaC**. Sometimes it is **CiCiC**, but the suffixes and stress patterns are the same. For example, the conjugation of **fihim** 'he understood' is

(ána)	fihímt	(íHna)	fihímna
(ínta)	fihímt	(íntu)	fihímtu
(ínti)	fihímti	(húmma)	fíhimu
(húwwa)	fíhim		
(híyya)	fíhimit		

Verbal Negatives

The negative structure for the perfect tense is **ma** + verb + **š**:

makatábtiš	*I didn't write*
makatábtiš	*you* (m.s.) *didn't write*
makatabtíiš	*you* (f.s.) *didn't write*
makatábš	*he didn't write*
makatabítš	*she didn't write*
makatabnáaš	*we didn't write*
makatabtúuš	*you* (pl.) *didn't write*
makatabúuš	*they didn't write*

Note that where there is already a cluster of two consonants before the **-š** suffix, the vowel **-i-** is added between the cluster and the suffix (e.g. **makatábtiš**). Where the addition of **š** creates a cluster of two consonants there is a shift in stress (e.g. **kátab** but **makatábš**). And where the form of the verb (before adding the negative structure) ends in a vowel, that vowel is lengthened and stressed (e.g. **makatabnáaš**).

Learn the following verbs and practise conjugating them in the perfect tense. Then practise the negative forms.

dáras	*to study*	ṭíli9	*to go up*
9ámal	*to make, do*	ḍárab	*to strike*
'áfal	*to close*	ṭálab	*to ask for*
nízil	*to descend*	dáxal	*to enter*
líbis	*to wear*	xárag	*to go out*
9írif	*to know*	'á9ad	*to stay, sit*
fátaH	*to open*	sákan	*to reside, live*

Active Participles (Simple Verbs)

Active participles have been previously introduced [Lesson 5] as having the form of adjectives but verbal meaning. Active participles of this type are usually made plural with the sound plural ending (**-iin**).

Active participles may also occur as nouns in which case the plural is often formed according to one of the broken plural patterns. Some can be used both adjectivally and nominally. For example:

	m.	*f.*	*pl.*	
(adj.)	9áamil	9ámla	9amlíin	= [*is/are*] *doing*
(n.)	9áamil	9ámla	9ummáal	= *labourer, workman*
(adj.)	káatib	kátba	katbíin	= [*is/are*] *writing*
(n.)	káatib	kátba	kuttáab	= *writer*

Compare the following:

in-naas dool 9amlíin Háaga g̲h̲aríiba	*Those people are doing something strange.*
in-naas dool 9ummáal	*Those people are labourers.*
in-naas dool katbíin asamíihum	*Those people are writing their names.*
in-naas dool kuttáab	*Those people are writers.*

Passive Participles (Simple Verbs)

The pattern for forming passive participles from simple verbs is **maCCuuC** (m.s.); **maCCuuCa** (f.s.); the plural is usually **maCCuCiin**, but sometimes a broken plural applies.

maktúub	*written*
maftúuH	*open*
mamnúu9	*forbidden*
masmúuH	*permitted*
mabsúuṭ	*happy*
maẓbúuṭ	*all right*
mašg̲h̲úul (mašg̲h̲ulíin)	*busy*
magnúun (maganíin)	*crazy, mad*

mafhúum	*understood; of course!*
mašhúur	*famous*

Additional vocabulary

líssa	*still; not yet* (with neg.)
ṣáaHib (aṣHáab)	*friend*
naháar	*daytime*
ṭuul (n. or prep.)	*length*
ṭuul in-naháar	*all day*
bálad	*town, downtown*
nízil	*to descend, go down*
nízil maṣr	*to go to Cairo*
nízil il-bálad	*to go downtown*
nízil fi lukánḍa	*to stay in a hotel*
fustáan (fasatíin)	*dress*
Haríir	*silk*
maHáll (maHalláat)	*store*
9ašáan	*because*
gúwwa (prep.)	*in, inside*
háwa (m.)	*air*
muluxíyya	*Mulukhiyya, Jew's mallow* (an Egyptian vegetable)
táani	*again*
asanséer	*lift, elevator*
sign (sugúun)	*jail*
ši9r	*poetry*
maqáala (maqaláat)	*article*

III EXERCISES

1 Reading practice

iṭ-ṭulláab dárasu id-dars il-xáamis áwwil imbáariH.
líssa madarasúuš id-dars is-sáadis.
9amáltu eeh fil-maktába?
katábna gawabáat li-aṣHábna fi maṣr.
'a9ádti fil-beet ṭuul in-naháar?
ábadan! ána nizílt il-bálad wi-ṭalábt tálat fasatíin Haríir min

maHáll gidíid fi šáari9 silimáan báaša.
il-9ummáal ma'afalúuš il-baab lámma xáragu.
il-9árab mašhuríin liš-ši9r bitá9hum.
id-duktóor ṭíli9 foo' bil-asanséer.

2 Translation exercise

1. léela fátaHit iš-šibbáak 9ašáan gúwwa l-beet ma fihúuš háwa.
2. il-awláad mabsuṭíin 9ašáan iṭ-ṭabbáax 9ámal muluxíyya táani!
3. daxálna l-máṭ9am wi-9abdúllah ṭalab šaay min ig-garsóon. ána ma ṭalábtiš Háaga.
4. Hásan nízil maṣr má9a ṣáHbuh [ṣáaHib + uh].
5. sakántu fi faránsa 'abl il-Harb wálla ba9dáha?
6. We entered the room at 9:30.
7. Why didn't you study the lesson?
8. He's crazy! He struck a policeman and now he's in jail.
9. Our teacher wrote an article about [9an] the pyramids.
10. He didn't stay because he's busy.

LESSON EIGHT (id-dars it-táamin)

I COMMON EXPRESSIONS

1	id-dínya Harr	*It's hot*
2	id-dínya bard	*It's cold*
3	id-dínya ḍálma	*It's dark*
4	id-dínya bitmáṭṭar	*It's raining*
5	híyya di d-dínya	*That's life!* ('C'est la vie!')

Note

(1,2,3,4,5) **id-dínya** = the world. It derives from a root meaning 'to be low', so in the literal sense it means 'the world down here on earth' and is opposed to the world up there, i.e. heaven. Hence these phrases mean literally 'the world is hot, cold, dark, etc.' You should note that the reference does not have to be exclusively to the outdoors. It can be said of the temperature, etc. indoors, if appropriate.

II GRAMMAR

Imperfect Tense (Simple Verbs)

The imperfect tense of simple verbs is formed on the patterns (i) **yiCCiC**, (ii) **yiCCaC**, and (iii) **yuCCuC**. The final vowel of each is presented in brackets beside the verb to indicate which pattern should be followed.

Using **kátab**, **fíhim**, and **xárag** as paradigms for the three patterns, we have:

1 kátab (i) *to write*

(ána)	áktib	*I write, am writing, shall write*
(ínta)	tíktib	*you* (m.s.) *write*
(ínti)	tiktíbi	*you* (f.s.) *write*
(húwwa)	yíktib	*he writes*
(híyya)	tíktib	*she writes*
(íHna)	níktib	*we write*
(íntu)	tiktíbu	*you* (pl.) *write*
(húmma)	yiktíbu	*they write*

íktib	*Write!* (m.s.)
iktíbi	*Write!* (f.s.)
iktíbu	*Write!* (pl.)

2 fíhim (a) *to understand*

(ána)	áfham	*I understand, am understanding, shall understand*
(ínta)	tífham	*you* (m.s.) *understand*
(ínti)	tifhámi	*you* (f.s.) *understand*
(húwwa)	yífham	*he understands*
(híyya)	tífham	*she understands*
(íHna)	nífham	*we understand*

(íntu)	tifhámu	*you* (pl.) *understand*
(húmma)	yifhámu	*they understand*

ífham	*Understand!* (m.s.)
ifhámi	*Understand!* (f.s.)
ifhámu	*Understand!* (pl.)

3 xárag (u) *to go out*

(ána)	áxrug	*I go out, am going out, shall go out*
(ínta)	túxrug	*you* (m.s.) *go out*
(ínti)	tuxrúgi	*you* (f.s.) *go out*
(húwwa)	yúxrug	*he goes out*
(híyya)	túxrug	*she goes out*
(íHna)	núxrug	*we go out*
(íntu)	tuxrúgu	*you* (pl.) *go out*
(húmma)	yuxrúgu	*they go out*

úxrug	*Go out!* (m.s.)
uxrúgi	*Go out!* (f.s.)
uxrúgu	*Go out!* (pl.)

Note that the **ínta** and **híyya** forms of the imperfect are identical.

In Egyptian Arabic the imperfect is usually preceded by **b(i)-** to denote the present and by **H(a)-** to denote the future.

báktib		Háktib
bitíktib		Hatíktib
bitiktíbi		Hatiktíbi
biyíktib	and	Hayíktib
bitíktib		Hatíktib
biníktib		Haníktib
bitiktíbu		Hatiktíbu
biyiktíbu		Hayiktíbu

The negative of the imperfect can be formed in three ways:

maktíbš	or	mabaktíbš/ maHaktíbš	or miš báktib/miš Háktib
matiktíbš		etc.	etc.
matiktibíiš			

mayiktíbš
matiktíbš
maniktíbš
matiktibúuš
mayiktibúuš

IMPORTANT: the negative imperative is based not on the imperative but on the imperfect indicative.

matiktíbš	*Don't write!* (m.s.)
matiktibíiš	*Don't write!* (f.s.)
matiktibúuš	*Don't write!* (pl.)

Here again are the verbs that appeared in Lesson Seven, this time followed by the vowels which indicate the pattern each verb follows for the imperfect. Carefully work through the list putting the verbs into the imperfect, negative imperfect, imperative and negative imperative.

dáras	(i)	ṭíli9	(a)
9ámal	(i)	ḍárab	(a)
'áfal	(i)	ṭálab	(u)
nízil	(i)	dáxal	(u)
líbis	(i)	'á9ad	(u)
9írif	(a)	sákan	(u)
fátaH	(a)		

The basic imperfect form of the verb (i.e., without prefixes **bi-** and **Ha-**) may be used (a) after certain active participles:

9áarif áktib 9árabi	*I know how to write Arabic.*
9áyza tínzil bil-asanséer	*She wants to take the lift down.*

and (b) after certain invariable auxiliaries like **láazim** and **ḍarúuri** (it is necessary), **miš láazim** and **miš ḍarúuri** (it is not necessary), **múmkin**, **yímkin** and **gáayiz** (it is possible), **mafrúuḍ** (supposed to):

láazim tílbis bi-súr9a	*You must get dressed in a hurry.*
mafrúuḍ tú'9ud hína	*You are supposed to sit here.*

'ga'

There are very few irregular verbs in Egyptian Arabic. Here is an important one: ga (to come)

	Perfect tense	*Negative*	*Imperfect*	*Imperative*
(ána)	geet	magítš	áagi	
(ínta)	geet	magítš	tíigi	ta9áala
(ínti)	géeti	magitíiš	tíigi	ta9áali
(húwwa)	ga	magáaš	yíigi	
(híyya)	gat	magátš	tíigi	
(íHna)	géena	maginéaš	níigi	
(íntu)	géetu	magitúuš	tíigu	ta9áalu
(húmma)	gum	magúuš	yíigu	

Additional vocabulary

taríix	*history*
riyaḍiyyáat	*mathematics*
9ilm (9ulúum)	*science*
Hanṭúur	*buggy, carriage (horse-driven)*
durg	*drawer*
musíiqa	*music*
wáagib	*duty; homework*
dáyya'	*narrow; short (time)*
ba9ḍ	*each other*
rígi9 (a) (without prep.)	*to return* (to)
šírib (a)	*to drink*
sími9 (a)	*to listen to, hear*
dáfa9 (a)	*to push; to pay*

Some new expressions based on the above vocabulary are:

ḍárab tilifóon li 9ámal tilifóon li	*to phone* [s.o.]
šírib sigáara	*to smoke*

III EXERCISES

1 Reading practice

ána báfham faransáawi šwáyya.
Hatúṭlub eeh fil-máṭ9am? ána Háṭlub gíbna béeḍa wi-9eeš báladi wi-fuul wi-zatúun.
ínta wi-mṛáatak bitidrísu eeh fig-gám9a, taríix wálla lug͟háat?
íHna mabnidríšš la taríix wala lug͟háat. ána bádris riyaḍiyyáat wi-mráati bitídris 9ulúum.
il-wa't dáyya'. írkab il-Hanṭúur w-írga9 il-lukánḍa.
il-Hisáab? wala yhímmak. miš ḍarúuri tídfa9 il-Hisáab innaharda. Múmkin tídfa9 búkra aw ba9d búkra.
law samáHt, údxul il-máktab bitáa9i w-í'fil id-durg.
húmma líssa mabyi9rafúuš ba9ḍ.

2 Translation exercise

1. ána básma9 musíiqa 9arabíyya.
2. híyya bitífham 9árabi kwáyyis.
3. gúzha mabyu'9údš fil-máktab bitáa9u. miš 9árfa húwwa feen.
4. iṭ-ṭulláab biyiktíbu l-wáagib bitá9hum. ínta Hatíktib il-wáagib bitáa9ak ímta?
5. di l-maHáṭṭa bitá9tak. ínzil bi-súr9a!
6. What do you (f.) want to drink?
7. They will live in Egypt for [a period of] three months.
8. It's not possible for me to return home before Friday.
9. Don't hit that boy! He's smaller than you are.
10. She went out a little while ago, but she will return in [after] five minutes.

LESSON NINE
(id-dars it-táasi9)

I COMMON EXPRESSIONS

1		kull sána w-ínta ṭáyyib (to m.s.) kull sána w-ínti ṭayyíba (to f.s.) kull sána w-íntu ṭayyibíin (to pl.)	*Season's greetings*
	(resp.)	w-ínta ṭáyyib etc.	*Same to you*
2		Hagg mabrúur	*Congratulations on your recent pilgrimage*
3		ramaḍáan karíim aḷḷáahu ákram	(See Note 3 below)

Notes

(1) Used by Muslims and Christians at any time of festive annual holiday, public or personal. Lit. = 'Every year and you are good'.
(2) Pilgrimage to Mecca is one of the so-called Five Pillars of Islam. Muslims should go on pilgrimage at least once in a lifetime. Lit. = 'Blessed pilgrimage'.
(3) Another Pillar of Islam is the annual fast for the month of Ramadan. Muslims observing the fast do not eat, drink or smoke from just before dawn until just after sunset for the whole month. Since the Islamic calendar is lunar, with a year about eleven days shorter than our fixed solar year, Ramadan gradually moves through the seasons. When it falls in summer the fast is longer and more difficult, but whatever the degree of severity it is always downplayed with the expression **ramaḍáan karíim**, which means 'Ramadan is generous'. **aḷḷáahu ákram** means 'God is more generous'.

The three other Pillars of Islam are:

– iš-šaháada	Lit. = 'bearing witness'. This is the profession of faith by saying: **laa iláaha ílla ḷḷaah, wa muHámmadun rasúulu-ḷḷaah**.
– iṣ-ṣaláah	The set prayer required five times daily (dawn, noon, mid-afternoon, sunset, and evening).
– iz-zakáah	Almsgiving.

II GRAMMAR

Doubled Verbs

In the perfect tense, simple doubled verbs take the form **CaCC**, the last two consonants being identical. The variable vowel for the imperfect may be **u** or **i**.

Haṭṭ (u) *to put*

	perfect	*imperfect*	*imperative*
(ána)	Haṭṭéet	aHúṭṭ	–
(ínta)	Haṭṭéet	tiHúṭṭ	Huṭṭ
(ínti)	Haṭṭéeti	tiHúṭṭi	Húṭṭi
(húwwa)	Haṭṭ	yiHúṭṭ	–
(híyya)	Háṭṭit	tiHúṭṭ	–
(íHna)	Haṭṭéena	niHúṭṭ	–
(íntu)	Haṭṭéetu	tiHúṭṭu	Húṭṭu
(húmma)	Háṭṭu	yiHúṭṭu	–

Conjugated like **Haṭṭ**:

radd	(u)	*to reply to* (9ala)
xašš	(u)	*to enter*
baṣṣ	(u)	*to look*
naṭṭ	(u)	*to jump*

9add (i) *to count*

	perfect	*imperfect*	*imperative*
(ána)	9addéet	a9ídd	–
(ínta)	9addéet	ti9ídd	9idd
(ínti)	9addéeti	ti9íddi	9íddi
(húwwa)	9add	yi9ídd	–
(híyya)	9áddit	ti9ídd	–
(íHna)	9addéena	ni9ídd	–
(íntu)	9addéetu	ti9íddu	9íddu
(húmma)	9áddu	yi9íddu	–

Conjugated like **9add**

Habb	(i)	*to like or love*
rann	(i)	*to ring*
Hagg	(i)	*to go on pilgrimage*
ghašš	(i)	*to cheat*

Hollow Verbs

Hollow verbs take the form **CaaC** in the perfect. The **aa** takes the place of a middle radical (either **w** or **y**) which is suppressed in conjugated forms of the simple verb (Form 1), but which does appear in the active participle and some of the derived forms. Notice particularly how the vowels change in the perfect. The variable vowels in the imperfect are **uu**, **ii**, or **aa**.

raaH (u) *to go*

	perfect	*imperfect*	*imperative*
(ána)	ruHt	arúuH	–
(ínta)	ruHt	tirúuH	ruuH
(ínti)	rúHti	tirúuHi	rúuHi
(húwwa)	raaH	yirúuH	–
(híyya)	ráaHit	tirúuH	–
(íHna)	rúHna	nirúuH	–
(íntu)	rúHtu	tirúuHu	rúuHu
(húmma)	ráaHu	yirúuHu	–

Conjugated like **raaH**:

'aal	(u)	*to say*
ṣaam	(u)	*to fast*
šaaf	(u)	*to see*
zaar	(u)	*to visit*
kaan	(u)	*to be*

gaab (i) *to bring*

	perfect	*imperfect*	*imperative*
(ána)	gibt	agíib	–
(ínta)	gibt	tigíib	giib
(ínti)	gíbti	tigíibi	gíibi
(húwwa)	gaab	yigíib	–
(híyya)	gáabit	tigíib	–
(íHna)	gíbna	nigíib	–
(íntu)	gíbtu	tigíibu	gíibu
(húmma)	gáabu	yigíibu	–

Conjugated like **gaab**:

šaal	(i)	*to carry*
baa9	(i)	*to sell*

naam (a) *to sleep, go to sleep*

	perfect	*imperfect*	*imperative*
(ána)	nimt	anáam	–
(ínta)	nimt	tináam	naam
(ínti)	nímti	tináami	náami
(húwwa)	naam	yináam	–
(híyya)	náamit	tináam	–
(íHna)	nímna	ninaám	–
(íntu)	nímtu	tináamu	náamu
(húmma)	náamu	yináamu	–

A variation on the above pattern is **xaaf (a) min** 'to be afraid of', which takes **u** instead of **i** in the first syllable of the perfect: **xuft** 'I feared'. The imperfect is regular: **axáaf**, **tixáaf**, etc.

Verbs with Weak Third Radical

ráma (i) *to throw*

	perfect	*imperfect*	*imperative*
(ána)	raméet	ármi	–
(ínta)	raméet	tírmi	írmi
(ínti)	raméeti	tírmi	írmi
(húwwa)	ráma	yírmi	–
(híyya)	rámit	tírmi	–
(íHna)	raméena	nírmi	–
(íntu)	raméetu	tírmu	írmu
(húmma)	rámu	yírmu	–

Conjugated like **ráma**:

káwa (i) *to iron*

A variation is **'ára (a)** 'to read', where there is an **a** in the place of the final **i** of the imperfect and imperative: **á'ra, tí'ra, yí'ra**, etc.

nísi (a) *to forget*

	perfect	*imperfect*	*imperative*
(ána)	nisíit	ánsa	–
(ínta)	nisíit	tínsa	ínsa
(ínti)	nisíiti	tínsi	ínsi
(húwwa)	nísi	yínsa	–
(híyya)	nísyit	tínsa	–
(íHna)	nisíina	nínsa	–
(íntu)	nisíitu	tínsu	ínsu
(húmma)	nísyu	yínsu	–

Conjugated like **nísi**:

ṣíHi (a) *to wake up*

Verbs like **míši (i)** 'to walk, go' and **gíri (i)** 'to run' take an **i** in the second syllable of both the imperfect and the imperative (perfect: **mišíit**, but imperfect: **ámši**, **tímši**, etc.).

Additional vocabulary

9iid il-miláad	*Christmas*
9iid il-'iyáama	*Easter*
9iid il-fiṭr	*Feast on 1 Shawwaal celebrating the end of the Ramadan Fast*
9iid il-áḍHa	*The so-called Feast of Immolation on 10 Zu l-Hijja*
9ašúura	*Ashura, on 10 Muharram, a voluntary fast day*
móolid in-nábi	*the Prophet's birthday*
šamm in-nisíim	*an Egyptian spring holiday on the Monday following Coptic Easter*
Hagg (Hugáag)	*pilgrim*
Higg	*pilgrimage*
ṣoom	*fast*
ṣáayim	*fasting*
il-'ál9a	*the Citadel*
il-mátHaf il-isláami	*the Islamic Museum*
abu l-hool	*the Sphinx*
g̲h̲eeṭ	*field*

III EXERCISES

1 Verb translation

Translate the following:

1. zúuru ábu l-hool!
2. magabítš il-Haláawa.
3. biynáam bádri.
4. buṣṣ hináak!
5. 'áalit kida.
6. matruHíiš li-wáHdik!
7. bitšúufi 9áadil.
8. báṣHa wáxri.
9. binHíbb maṣr.
10. 'uul!
11. mansáaš il-asáami.

12. rúddi 9a t-tilifóon!
13. matnamíiš 9ála l-arḍ!
14. HarúuH ispáanya.
15. biyšíil is-sábat.
16. Hanímši sáwa.
17. bi9t iš-šá''a.
18. 'aréet il-maqáala.
19. ána xuft mínnuh.
20. ígri!
21. máaši
22. Háaṭiṭ
23. rayHíin
24. ṣáayim
25. náyma

2 *Translation exercise*

1. ig-garsóon gaab fingáan 'áhwa.
2. láazim ašúuf id-duktóor wi húwwa fil-mustášfa.
3. Huséen šaaf il-bint di fig-gám9a wi ba9d šwáyya ána šuft nafs il-bint fil-máṭ9am.
4. nagíib biyHíbb in-noom – biynáam bádri wi-biyíṣHa wáxri.
5. raddéeti 9ála gawáabuh wálla líssa?
6. Did you visit the Islamic Museum or the citadel?
7. They fasted in the month of Ramadan.
8. The farmer carried the boy to the fields.
9. Bring your suitcase with you.
10. Where do you (pl.) want to go on Saturday afternoon?

LESSON TEN
(id-dars il-9áašir)

I COMMON EXPRESSIONS

1	bil-hána wiš-šífa	(See Note 1 below)
(resp.)	aḷḷáah yihanníik	

	aḷḷáah yihanníiki	
	aḷḷáah yihanníikum	
2	haníyyan	(See Note 2 below)
(resp.)	hannáak aḷḷáah	
3	súfra dáyma	(See Note 3 below)
(resp.)	yidúum 9ízzak	

Notes

(1) Said by you as host when a guest compliments you on the food you are serving. Lit. = 'To [your] happiness and health' and (resp.) 'May God give you happiness'.
(2) Said by you after someone drinks. Lit. = 'In happiness' and (resp.) 'May God give you happiness', an alternative to **aḷḷáah yihanníik**.
(3) Said by guest after eating at someone's house. Lit. = 'May your dining table be always thus' and (resp.) 'May your honour [and good standing] last always'.

II GRAMMAR

Pronominal Suffixes as Direct Objects

We have seen the pronominal suffixes used as possessive pronouns and as objects of prepositions. They may also be attached to verbs, as direct objects, in which case the suffixes are the same with the exception of the 1st person singular which changes to **-ni**.

fihímni	*he understood me*	šáfni	*he saw me*
fíhimak	*he understood you* (m.)	šáafak	*etc*
fíhimik	*he understood you* (f.)	šáafik	
fíhimuh	*he understood him/it*	šáafuh	
fihímha	*he understood her/it*	šáfha	
fihímna	*he understood us*	šáfna	
fihímkum	*he understood you* (pl.)	šáfkum	
fihímhum	*he understood them*	šáfhum	

When the basic verb already ends in two consonants, a suffix that begins with a consonant must be preceded by a helping vowel.

fihimtíni	*you* (s.) *understood me*
fihímtak	*I understood you* (m.)
fihímtik	*I understood you* (f.)
fihímtuh	*I* or *you understood him/it*
fihimtáha	*I* or *you understood her/it*
fihimtína	*you* (s.) *understood us*
fihimtúkum	*I understood you* (pl.)
fihimtúhum	*I* or *you understood them*

When the basic verb ends in a vowel, that vowel must be made long when adding a suffix.

fihimnáah	*we understood him*
šafúukum	*they saw you* (pl.)
biyifhamúuha	*they understand her*
mayifhamuháaš	*they do not understand her*

Study the following paradigm for the 3rd pers.m.s. suffix (**-uh**) attached to the complete conjugation in the perfect of **kátab**.

(ána)	katábtuh	(íHna)	katabnáah
(ínta)	katábtuh	(íntu)	katabtúuh
(ínti)	katabtíih	(húmma)	katabúuh
(húwwa)	kátabuh		
(híyya)	katabítuh		

This 3rd pers. m.s. suffix changes when attached to a negative verb and itself followed by the negative suffix **-š**. The following patterns are both common among native speakers.

(ána)	makatabtuhúuš	*or*	makatabtúuš
(ínta)	makatabtuhúuš		makatabtúuš
(ínti)	makatabtihúuš		makatabtíiš
(húwwa)	makatabhúuš		makatabúuš
(híyya)	makatabithúuš		makatabitúuš
(íHna)	makatabnahúuš		makatabnáaš
(íntu)	makatabtuhúuš		makatabtúuš
(húmma)	makatabuhúuš		makatabúuš

It is recommended that you learn to understand both patterns. For your own speech the first pattern may be preferable as there is less inherent ambiguity. For example, **makatabúuš** (from the second pattern) might mean 'he did not write it', 'they did not write it', or 'they did not write'.

Relative clauses

In English a relative clause is a dependent clause that begins with 'that', 'which', 'who', etc. (e.g. The book which I read was expensive.). The structure of Arabic relative clauses differs depending on whether the antecedent is definite or indefinite. If it is definite the relative pronoun is **ílli**.

iṛ-ṛáagil ílli kátab il-gawáab da . . .	*The man who wrote that letter . . .*
is-sitt ílli fil-beet . . .	*The lady who is at home . . .*

If the antecedent is indefinite the relative pronoun must be omitted.

lazímna wáHda sitt Hatúṭbux lína l-akl	*We need some lady who will cook for us.*
fiih mudárris biyíḍrab talamíizuh	*There is a teacher who beats his students.*

If the antecedent is the object of a verb or preposition in the relative clause, a pronominal suffix agreeing with the antecedent must appear in the relative clause.

id-dars ílli darástuh . . .	*The lesson that I studied . . .*
il-lukánḍa lli nizílt fíiha	*The hotel where I stayed . . .*

III EXERCISE

Read carefully the example sets of questions and answers, then continue the exercise by completing the answers for 1 to 4 yourself.

(example) dafá9t il-Hisáab bitáa9 il-kahrába?
áywa, dafá9tuh.
la, madafa9tuhúuš.

(example) šúftu l-film ig-gidíid fi sínima 'aṣr in-niil?
áywa, šufnáah.
la, mašufnahúuš.

(example)	šuftíina fil-masraH imbáariH? áywa, šuftúku. la, mašuftukúuš.
(example)	il-makwági káwa l-'amíiṣ? áywa, kawáah. la, makawahúuš.
1.	fatáHt iš-šibbáak? áywa, ... la, ...
2.	gíbtu l-gawáab? áywa, ... la, ...
3.	zurtína fiš-šíta aw fir-rabíi9 issána lli fáatit? . . . . fiš-šíta. ma . . . . fir-rabíi9.
4.	il-wálad ráma l-'álam? áywa, ... la, ...

LESSON ELEVEN (id-dars il-Hidáašar)

I COMMON EXPRESSIONS

1		šidd Héelak (to m.s.)	*Be strong*
	or	šíddi Héelik (to f.s.)	
	or	šíddu Hélkum (to pl.)	
	(resp.)	iš-šídda 9ála ḷḷaah	
2		rabbína yisáhhil	*May our Lord make [it] easy*
3		aḷḷáah yi'awwíik, etc.	*May our Lord make you strong*

4	salámtak	*I hope you feel better soon*
	salámtik	
	salamítkum	
(resp.)	a̤l̤láah yisallímak, etc.	*Thank you*

Notes

(1) Said to someone facing difficulty or mental anguish – anything from too much work to a situation of mourning. More literally: 'Pull yourself together'. Resp.: 'Strength [depends] on God', i.e., we leave the dispensing of strength to God.
(2) As (1) above, said to someone facing difficulty.
(3) As (1) above.
(4) Said to someone who is ill. **saláama** here means 'good health'.

II GRAMMAR

The derived forms

Verbal forms II to X are called the 'derived forms'. You should recognise many of the same root letter combinations that appear in the simple form of the verb (Form 1). A given set of root letters may appear in one or several verbal forms but hardly ever in all ten forms.

		patterns	examples	
Form II		CaCCaC	fákkar	*to think; to remind*
	(or)	CaCCiC	fáhhim	*to make s.o. understand*
Form III		CaaCiC	sáafir	*to travel*
Form IV		aCCaC	áḍrab	*to go on strike*
Form V		itCaCCaC	itfárrag 9ála	*to look at*
	(or)	itCaCCiC	itHássin	*to get better*
Form VI		itCaaCiC	itfáahim má9a	*to reach an understanding (with)*
Form VII		inCaCaC	inbásaṭ	*to enjoy oneself*

Form VIII		iCtaCaC	ibtásam	*to smile*
Form IX		iCCaCC	iHmárr	*to become red*
Form X		istaCCaC	istághrab	*to be surprised*
	(or)	istaCCiC	istá9mil	*to use*

Verbal Form II (CaCCaC or **CaCCiC)**

Often denotes:
1 causation (e.g. **maat** 'to die'; **máwwit** 'to cause to die, to kill')
2 intensity (e.g. **'áṭa9** 'to cut'; **'áṭṭa9** 'to cut into many pieces')

9állim *to teach*

	perfect	*imperfect*	*imperative*
(ána)	9allímt	a9állim	–
(ínta)	9allímt	ti9állim	9állim
(ínti)	9allímti	ti9allími	9allími
(húwwa)	9állim	yi9állim	–
(híyya)	9allímit	ti9állim	–
(íHna)	9allímna	ni9állim	–
(íntu)	9allímtu	ti9allímu	9allímu
(húmma)	9allímu	yi9allímu	–

Form II verbs which have **a** as the second vowel are conjugated the same way (e.g. **fákkar** 'to think' (Perfect: **fakkárt**; and Imperfect: **afákkar**, etc.)

Like **9állim** and **fákkar**:

kállim	*to speak to*
kábbar	*to enlarge*
ṣállaH	*to repair*
Háḍḍar	*to prepare*
fáḍḍal	*to prefer*
máwwit	*to kill*
fáhhim	*to explain*

Form II verbs with a weak third radical have a conjugation in the perfect similar to that of the simple doubled verbs. The imperfect and imperative are regular:

wárra *to show*

	perfect	*imperfect*	*imperative*
(ána)	warréet	awárri	–
(ínta)	warréet	tiwárri	wárri
(ínti)	warréeti	tiwárri	wárri
(húwwa)	wárra	yiwárri	–
(híyya)	wárrit	tiwárri	–
(íHna)	warréena	niwárri	–
(íntu)	warréetu	tiwárru	wárru
(húmma)	wárru	yiwárru	–

Like **wárra**:

rábba	*to raise, bring up*
ṣálla	*to pray*
xábba	*to hide (s.th.), conceal*
wádda	*to take (to a place), deliver*
9ádda	*to cross; exceed*

Verbal Form III (CaaCiC)

Usually denotes effort, often effort to do something to or for someone.

sáafir *to travel*

	perfect	*imperfect*	*imperative*
(ána)	safírt	asáafir	–
(ínta)	safírt	tisáafir	sáafir
(ínti)	safírti	tisáfri	sáfri
(húwwa)	sáafir	yisáafir	–
(híyya)	sáfrit	tisáafir	–
(íHna)	safírna	nisáafir	–
(íntu)	safírtu	tisáfru	sáfru
(húmma)	sáfru	yisáfru	–

Like **sáafir**:

'áabil	*to meet*
záakir	*to study*
sáa9id	*to help*
Háawil	*to try, attempt*
gáawib	*to answer*

The pattern for Form III verbs with a weak third radical:

náada *to call out to*

	perfect	*imperfect*	*imperative*
(ána)	nadéet	anáadi	–
(ínta)	nadéet	tináadi	náadi
(ínti)	nadéeti	tináadi	náadi
(húwwa)	náada	yináadi	–
(híyya)	náadit	tináadi	–
(íHna)	nadéena	nináadi	–
(íntu)	nadéetu	tináadi	náadu
(húmma)	náadu	yináadu	–

Like **náada**:

láa'a *to meet s.o.*

Verbal Form IV (aCCaC)

Form IV verbs are generally causative in Classical Arabic. Colloquial Arabic prefers Form II to denote causation which makes Form IV rare in the Colloquial. However, you will encounter many Form IV active participles.

áḍrab *to go on strike*

	perfect	*imperfect*	*imperative*
(ána)	aḍrábt	áḍrib	–
(ínta)	aḍrábt	tíḍrib	íḍrib
(ínti)	aḍrábti	tiḍríbi	iḍríbi
(húwwa)	áḍrab	yíḍrib	–
(híyya)	aḍrábit	tíḍrib	–

(íHna)	aḍrábna	níḍrib	–
(íntu)	aḍrábtu	tiḍríbu	iḍríbu
(húmma)	aḍrabu	yiḍríbu	–

Like **adrab**:

ásbat (yísbit)	*to prove*
ákram (yíkrim)	*to be hospitable to*
áslam (yíslam)	*to become a Muslim*

(Note the **a** in **yíslam**)

Participles

The following words are all participles of derived verbs. In Classical Arabic the first syllable of the participial patterns is always **mu-**; in some Colloquial words this becomes **mi-**. Active participles take **i** as a final vowel. Passive participles take **a**.

Form II	mu9állim	*teacher*
	mudárris	*teacher*
	mufáttiš	*inspector*
	mufáḍḍal	*preferred*
Form III	musáa9id	*helper, assistant*
	misáafir	*travelling, traveller*
	muHáasib	*accountant*
Form IV	múslim	*Muslim*
	mudíir	*director, manager*
	mufíid	*useful*
	múdhiš	*wonderful*

III EXERCISES

1 Substitute the forms given below, making any necessary changes to the sentence:

1. ínta bitfákkar fi eeh?
   húwwa . . . .?
   húmma . . . .?

2. ana bafáḍḍal il-bíira 9ála n-nibíit.
ínta . . . .
íHna . . . .

3. láazim ag̲h̲áyyir hudúumi bi-súr9a.
(híyya) . . . .
(íntu) . . . .

4. waldítuh sáfrit aswáan yoom il-itnéen, miš kída?
wálduh . . . .?
agdáaduh . . . .?

5. nádya bitdárris 9árabi wálla ingilíizi?
Hásan . . . .?
nádya wi-Hásan . . . .?

Additional vocabulary

Háyya (Hayyáat)	*viper*
bíira	*beer*
nibíit	*wine*
hudúum	*clothes*
wáalid	(= abb) *father*
wálda	(= umm) *mother*

2 Make the appropriate changes to the sentences below:

1. il-falláaH Háawil yimáwwit il-Háyya.
il-fallaHíin . . . .

2. il-mudarrísa bitfáhhim iṭ-ṭulláab id-dars.
il-mudarrisíin . . . .

3. iṭ-ṭabbáax biyHáḍḍar il-9áša.
iṭ-ṭabbaxíin . . . .

4. il-9áamil da miš Hayíḍrib.
il-9ummáal dool . . . .

LESSON TWELVE
(id-dars il-itnáašar)

A principal character of Middle Eastern folk literature is Goha. Usually depicted riding a donkey or quarrelling with his nagging wife, Goha plays the fool but always gets the last laugh. These stories are ideal for learning Arabic so see if you can learn them by heart. The translations are included in the Exercise Key.

I

márra kaan gúHa 'áa9id taHt šágarit búndu', wa 'á9ad yifákkar fi eeh il-Híkma ínnu rabbína yixálli šágara kibíira tíṭraH búndu' ṣugháyyar wi-yixálli l-baṭṭíix ílli húwwa ákbar min il-búndu' luh far9 ṣugháyyar mayi'dárš yišíiluh. min kutr it-tafkíir gúHa naam, wi-ba9déen ṣíHi maxḍúuḍ 9ála búndu'a wí'i9it 9ála ṛáasuh. fa-'aal il-Hámdu lilláah ya rábbi. 9iríft Hikmítak inn iš-šágara l-kibíira di mabtiṭráHiš baṭṭíix kaan zamáani ruHt fašúuš.

Vocabulary

márra	*once*
'áa9id	*sitting*
šágara (ašgáar)	*tree*
búndu'	*hazel-nuts* (collective)
búndu'a	*hazel-nut* (s.)
'á9ad yifákkar	*he went on thinking*
Híkma	*wisdom*
ínnu	*that*
rabb	*Lord*
xálli, yixálli	*to let*
táraH, yíṭraH	*to give forth*
baṭṭíix	*water-melon*
luh	*it has*
far9 (furúu9)	*branch*
'ídir, yí'dar	*to be able*
šaal, yišíil	*to carry*

kutr	*large quantity*
tafkíir (v.n.)	*thinking*
ba9déen	*afterwards*
maxḍúuḍ 9ála	*startled by*
wí'i9, yú'a9	*to fall*
kaan zamáani ruHt fašuuš	(very idiomatic) *'it would have been curtains for me'*

II

márra wi-gúHa máaši, il-9iyáal 'á9adu yi9aksúuh. fa-9ašáan yitxállaṣ mínhum 'alláhum ínnu fiih 9izúuma fi beet ṣáHbuh il-Hagg 9áli. il-9iyáal ma saddá'u ráaHu ṭal9íin gíru délhum fi sinánhum. ba9d ma ráaHu gúHa fákkar 'aal ma gáayiz yikúun fiih 9izúuma bi-ṣaHíiH wi-ṭíli9 yígri húwwa kamáan 9ála beet il-Hagg 9áli.

Vocabulary

9iyáal (= wiláad)	*children*
9áakis, yi9áakis	*to tease*
'á9adu yi9aksúuh	*[they] went on teasing him*
itxállaṣ, yitxállaṣ min	*to get rid of*
'alláhum (= 'aal + la + hum)	*he said to them*
9izúuma (= Háfla)	*party*
ma saddá'u	*no sooner believed than*
deel	*tail (here the hems of their galabias)*
sinn (sináan)	*teeth*
ma gáayiz yikúun fiih	*maybe there is*
bi-ṣaHíiH	*truly, really*
gíri, yígri 9ála	*to run to*

LESSON THIRTEEN (id-dars it-talaṭṭáašar)

I COMMON EXPRESSIONS

1		na9íiman	*You look refreshed*
	(resp.)	án9am aḷḷáah 9aléek, etc.	*Thank you*
2		mášaḷḷaah	(See note below)

Notes

(1) Said to someone who is looking refreshed after a shower, shave, hair-cut, etc. Lit. = '[May you be] in comfort' and (resp.) 'May God give you comfort'.

(2) or **ma šaa' aḷḷáah** Said when one sees something beautiful or admirable. Perhaps by now it has been said to you of your Arabic. It will certainly be said if you have a large family (à l'egyptienne) of your own. Lit. = 'That which God wills [is beautiful or admirable]'

II GRAMMAR

Verbal Form V (itCaCCaC or itCaCCiC)

The reflexive of Form II:
9állim 'to cause to know, to teach' → **it9állim** 'to cause oneself to know, to learn'

it9állim *to learn*

	perfect	*imperfect*	*imperative*
(ána)	it9allímt	at9állim	–
(ínta)	it9allímt	tit9állim	it9állim
(ínti)	it9allímti	tit9allími	it9allími
(húwwa)	it9állim	yit9állim	–
(híyya)	it9allímit	tit9állim	–
(íHna)	it9allímna	nit9állim	–
(íntu)	it9allímtu	tit9allímu	it9allímu
(húmma)	it9allímu	yit9allímu	–

like **it9allim**:

itgáwwiz, yitgáwwiz	*to get married*
itkállim, yitkállim má9a	*to speak (with)*
it'áxxar, yit'áxxar	*to be late*
itṣáwwar, yitṣáwwar	*to imagine*
itxárrag, yitxárrag	*to graduate*

Form V verbs with a weak third radical:

itg̲h̲ádda (itg̲h̲addéet), yitg̲h̲ádda	*to have lunch*
it9áššа (it9aššéet), yit9áššа	*to have dinner*

Verbal Form VI (itCaaCiC)

Usually the reflexive of Form III, often conveying an idea of reciprocity.

itfáahim (má9a) *to reach an understanding (with)*

	perfect	*imperfect*	*imperative*
(ána)	itfahímt	atfáahim	–
(ínta)	itfahímt	titfáahim	itfáahim
(ínti)	itfahímti	titfáhmi	itfáhmi
(húwwa)	itfáahim	yitfáahim	–
(híyya)	itfáhmit	titfáahim	–
(íHna)	itfahímna	nitfáahim	–
(íntu)	itfahímtu	titfáhmu	itfáhmu
(húmma)	itfáhmu	yitfáhmu	–

Like **itfáahim**:

it'áabil, yit'áabil	*to meet* (intrans.)
itnáa'iš, yitnáa'iš	*to discuss*
itxáani', yitxáani'	*to quarrel*

Sometimes the 't' of the pattern is assimilated into the first root letter.

iddáayi'	*to be annoyed*

Verbal Form VII (inCaCaC)

Reflexive of Form I

inbásaṭ *to enjoy o.s.*

	perfect	*imperfect*	*imperative*
(ána)	inbasáṭṭ	anbísiṭ	–
(ínta)	inbasáṭṭ	tinbísiṭ	inbísiṭ
(ínti)	inbasáṭṭi	tinbísṭi	inbísṭi
(húwwa)	inbásaṭ	yinbísiṭ	–
(híyya)	inbásaṭit	tinbísiṭ	–
(íHna)	inbasáṭna	ninbísiṭ	–
(íntu)	inbasáṭṭu	tinbísṭu	inbísṭu
(húmma)	inbásaṭu	yinbísṭu	–

Like **inbásaṭ**:

inkásar, yinkísir	*to break* (intrans.)
infátaH, yinfítiH	*to open* (intrans.)
insáHab, yinsíHib	*to withdraw* (intrans.)

Participles

Form V	mitgáwwiz	*married*
	mit'áxxar	*late, delayed*
	mitg̲h̲áyyar	*changed*
	mitg̲h̲áddi	*(have) lunched*
	mitšákkir	*thank you*
	mit'ássif	*sorry*
Form VI	mitšáa'im	*pessimistic*
	mitfáa'il	*optimistic*
	middáayi'	*annoyed*
Form VII	munfá9il	*upset, agitated*
	mundáhiš	*surprised*

III EXERCISES

1 Translate the following:

1. láazim nit9állim faransáawi.
2. Hatit'áblu feen?
3. híyya txárragit is-sána lli fáatit.
4. yímkin at'áxxar šwáyya.
5. aṣHábna nbasaṭu kitíir.
6. itkállim ma9áah.
7. matit'axxarúuš!
8. il-baab infátaH.
9. ána wi húwwa láazim nitfáahim má9a ba9ḍ.
10. il-miráaya nkásarit.

2 Make the appropriate changes:

1. muráad* dáyman biyit'áxxar!
húda** . . . . !
húmma . . . . !

2. ána Hatxárrag min ig-gám9a s-sanáadi, in šaa' aḷḷáah.
ínti . . . .
húwwa . . . .

3. il-fallaHíin láazim yit'áblu iṣ-ṣubH gamb in-niil.
íHna láazim . . . .
íntu láazim . . . .

4. ínta bitHíbb tit9ášša bádri wálla wáxri?
húmma . . . . ?
nabíila . . . . ?

5. iṭ-ṭáalib il-ingilíizi da ga maṣr 9ašáan yit9állim 9árabi.
iṭ-ṭaalíba . . . .
iṭ-ṭuḷḷáab . . . .

* boy's name
** girl's name

LESSON FOURTEEN
(id-dars il-arba9ṭáašar)

I COMMON EXPRESSIONS

1	ixs 9aléek, etc.	*Shame on you!*
2	Haráam 9aléek, etc.	*You must not do that. It's wrong!*
3	la sámaH aḷḷáah	*May God not permit it to happen!*
4	bi9d iš-šarr	*May evil be far away!*

Notes

(1) May be a light-hearted as well as a serious admonition.
(2) **Haraam** = that which is forbidden by Islam. The opposite is **Halaal**, that which is allowed by Islam.
(3 & 4) One or other of these expressions is used whenever any potential evil or unpleasantness is mentioned.

II GRAMMAR

Verbal Form VIII (iCtaCaC)

Also reflexive of Form I with the difference that Form VIII verbs may take a direct object.

ibtásam *to smile*

	perfect	*imperfect*	*imperative*
(ána)	ibtasámt	abtísim	–
(ínta)	ibtasámt	tibtísim	ibtísim
(ínti)	ibtasámti	tibtísmi	ibtísmi
(húwwa)	ibtásam	yibtísim	–
(híyya)	ibtásamit	tibtísim	–
(íHna)	ibtasámna	nibtísim	–
(íntu)	ibtasámtu	tibtísmu	ibtísmu
(húmma)	ibtásamu	yibtísmu	–

Like **ibtásam**:

iHtáram, yiHtírim	*to respect*
iftákar, yiftíkir	*to think*
istálam, yistílim	*to receive*
ištág͟hal, yištág͟hal	*to work (as)*

With a weak first radical:

ittáfa', yittífi' má9a	*to agree with*
iṭṭáṣal, yiṭṭíṣil bi	*to contact, get in touch with*

With a weak second radical:

ixtáar, yixtáar	*to choose*

With a weak third radical:

ištára (ištaréet), yištíri	*to buy*
ibtáda (ibtadéet), yibtídi	*to begin*

Verbal Form IX (iCCaCC)

The rarest of the derived forms; associated with adjectives denoting colour and physical disability.

(áHmar →) iHmárr *to become red; blush; get sunburned*

	perfect	*imperfect*	*imperative*
(ána)	iHmarréet	aHmárr	–
(ínta)	iHmarréet	tiHmárr	iHmárr
(ínti)	iHmarréeti	tiHmárri	iHmárri
(húwwa)	iHmárr	yiHmárr	–
(híyya)	iHmárrit	tiHmárr	–
(íHna)	iHmarréena	niHmárr	–
(íntu)	iHmarréetu	tiHmárru	iHmárru
(húmma)	iHmárru	yiHmárru	–

Like **iHmarr**:

(áxdar →)	ixḍárr, yixḍárr	*to turn green*
(áṣfar →)	iṣfárr, yiṣfárr	*to turn yellow*
(ásmar →)	ismárr, yismárr	*to get tanned*
(áṭraš →)	iṭrášš, yiṭrášš	*to become deaf*
(á9rag →)	i9rágg, yi9rágg	*to become lame*

Verbal Form X (istaCCaC or **istaCCiC)**

Usually denotes asking or doing for oneself; its least common use, considering (s.th. or s.o.) to be (s.th.) might also be its most amusing, as in **istáHmar**, **yistáHmar** to consider (s.o.) to be a donkey (= **Humáar**).

istá9mil *to use*

	perfect	*imperfect*	*imperative*
(ána)	ista9mílt	astá9mil	–
(ínta)	ista9mílt	tistá9mil	istá9mil
(ínti)	ista9mílti	tista9míli	ista9míli
(húwwa)	istá9mil	yistá9mil	–
(híyya)	istá9milit	tistá9mil	–
(íHna)	ista9mílna	nistá9mil	–
(íntu)	ista9míltu	tista9mílu	ista9mílu
(húmma)	istá9milu	yista9mílu	–

Like **istá9mil**:

	istá9gil, yistá9gil	*to hurry*
	istá'zin, yistá'zin	*to excuse o.s.*
	istálṭaf, yistálṭaf	*to consider (s.o.) nice*
(hollow)	ista'áal, yista'íil	*to resign*
(doubled)	ista9ádd (ist9addéet), yista9ídd	*to be ready*
(final weak)	istá9la (ista9léet), yistá9la	*to be stuffy or pompous*

Participles

Form VIII	muHtáram	*respected*
	muxtálif	*different*
Form IX	(rare)	
Form X	mistá9gil	*in a hurry*
	mistá9mal	*used, second-hand*
	musta9ídd	*ready*

Quadriliterals

Quadriliteral verbs have four root letters instead of the usual three, but their conjugation is perfectly consistent and regular. They follow exactly the pattern of Form II verbs (see Lesson Eleven).

	tárgim, yitárgim	*to translate*
	láxbaṭ, yiláxbaṭ	*to muddle*
(derived)	itláxbaṭ, yitláxbaṭ	*to be muddled*

Cultural note:
The word for 'translator' is **mutárgim (mutargimíin)**. The now archaic word **targumáan** derives from the same root, of course, and was the source for the also archaic English word 'dragoman' meaning 'guide/interpreter'.

III EXERCISES

1 Translate the following:

1. abúuya biyištághal ṣúHafi
2. Hatištíri eeh fi xaan il-xalíili?
3. léela iHmárrit min iš-šams
4. láazim nastá'zin dilwá'ti
5. Hásan ištára 9ágala gidíida
6. múmkin astá9mil il-qamúus bitáa9ak.
7. il-mušáa kullúhum mista9gilíin.

Vocabulary

mušáa	*pedestrians*
muHáami	*lawyer*
a9ḍáa' il-máglis	*the members of the Council*
masraHíyya	*(theatrical) play*
šeex (šuyúux)	*old man; Senator*
ra'íis il-wúzara	*Prime Minister*

2 Make the appropriate changes:

1. ána baštághal muHáami.
   húwwa . . . .
   ínta . . . .

2. il-mudíir Hayista'íil búkra.
   il-mudarrísa . . . .
   a9ḍáa' il-máglis . . . .

3. ána istalámt il-filúus min il-bank.
   híyya . . . .
   húmma . . . .

4. nagíib ištára tázkara lil-masraHíyya.
   ána . . . .
   miṛáati . . . .

5. iš-šeex muHtáram . . .
   iš-šuyúux . . . .
   ra'íisit il-wúzara . . . .

LESSON FIFTEEN
(id-dars il-xamasṭáašar)

I COMMON EXPRESSIONS

1		šarraftína (to m.s.)	*Very pleased to see you*
	or	šarraftíina (to f.s.)	
	or	šarraftúuna (to pl.)	
	(resp.)	aḷḷáh yišárraf mi'dáarak (to m.s.)	*Thank you*
		etc.	
2		nawwárt il-beet (to m.s.)	(As above)
	or	nawwárti l-beet (to f.s.)	
	or	nawwártu l-beet (to pl.)	
	(resp.)	aḷḷáah yináwwar 9aléek (to m.s.)	
		etc.	

3		anistína (to m.s.)	(As above)
	or	anistíina (to f.s.)	
	or	anistúuna (to pl.)	
	(resp.)	aḷḷáah yi'ánsak (to m.s.)	
	or	aḷḷáah yi'ánsik (to f.s.)	
	or	aḷḷáah yi'anískim (to pl.)	
4		waHíšni	*I miss you* (to m.)
		waHšáani	*I miss you* (to f.)
		waHaštíni	*I missed you* (to m.)
		waHášni	*I missed him*
		waHašúuni	*I missed them*
		HatiwHášni	*I shall miss you* (to m.)
	(resp.)	matšúfš wíHiš	(See below)
		matšufíiš wíHiš	

Notes

(1) Said to your guest. Lit. 'You have honoured us' and (resp.) 'May God honour you'.
(2) Same as (1) above. Lit. 'You have brought light to the house', i.e. to our house; (resp.) 'May God give you light'.
(3) Same as (1) and (2) above. Lit. 'You have cheered us up' and (resp.) 'May God cheer you'.
(4) Notice how the Arabic really says this the other way around: 'You are missed by me'. Resp. = 'May you not see [anything] bad!'

II GRAMMAR

Verbal Nouns

A verbal noun, called 'maṣdar' in Arabic, is a noun derived directly from a verb. When translated into English such a noun may appear as a gerund (i.e. the form of the verb which ends in '--ing' and is used as a noun, as in 'Running is good exercise'). Verbal nouns can be grouped by patterns, but for simple (Form 1) verbs these are too numerous to try to memorise. Each new example should simply be learned as a new item of vocabulary.

verb	*verbal noun*	*meaning*
kátab	kitáaba	*writing*
zaar	ziyáara	*visiting; visit*
dáxal	duxúul	*entering*
xárag	xurúug	*going out*
wíṣil	wuṣúul	*arriving; arrival*
ṭíli9	ṭulúu9	*ascending*
nízil	nuzúul	*descending*
dáras	dars	*lesson*
ḍárab	ḍarb	*striking*
fíhim	fahm	*understanding*
sákan	sákan	*dwelling*
šírib	šurb	*drinking*
kal	akl	*eating; food*
naam	noom	*sleeping*
míši	mášy	*walking*
ráma	rámy	*throwing*

Verbal noun patterns for the derived forms of the verb tend to be regular and predictable. The following examples give the basic patterns for 'sound' derived verbs.

II	9állim	ta9líim
	ṣállaH	taṣlíiH
III	sáa9id	musá9da
	Háawil	muHáwla
IV	áḍrab	iḍráab
	ákram	ikráam
V	it9állim	ta9állum
	itxáṣṣaṣ	taxáṣṣuṣ
VI	itfáahim	tafáahum
	it9áamil	ta9áamul

VII	insáHab	insiHáab
	inbásaṭ	inbisáaṭ
VIII	iHtáram	iHtiráam
	ištárak	ištiráak
IX	iHmárr	iHmiráar
X	istá9mil	isti9máal

Nouns of Place

Nouns of place generally occur on the patterns **maCCaC**, **maCCiC**, and **maCCaCa**. The plural is usually **maCaaCiC** for all three patterns.

kátab	máktab (makáatib)	*place of writing*	→ *office; desk*
ṭábax	máṭbax (maṭáabix)	*place of cooking*	→ *kitchen*
dáxal	mádxal (madáaxil)	*place of entering*	→ *entrance*
xárag	máxrag (maxáarig)	*place of exiting*	→ *exit*
ságad	másgid (masáagid)	*place of kneeling*	→ *mosque*
wí'if	máw'if (mawáa'if)	*place of stopping*	→ *(parking) place*
dáras	madrása (madáaris)	*place of studying*	→ *school*
kátab	maktába (maktabáat)	*place of writing*	→ *library; bookshop*
Hákam	maHkáma (maHáakim)	*place of judging*	→ *law-court*

The following are also nouns of place, but based on root forms possessing weak or doubled radicals.

ṭaar	maṭáar (maṭaráat)	*place of flying*	→ *airport*
kaan	makáan (amáakin)	*place of being*	→ *place*
Hatt	maHáṭṭa (maHaṭṭáat)	*place of putting down**	→ *station*

*From Classical Arabic where **Haṭṭ** has the additional meaning of alighting, or putting down.

Collective Nouns

Certain nouns (e.g., fruit, vegetables and animals) have a 'collective' form in addition to the usual singular and plural forms. The collective is general in scope in that it refers to the class of items as a whole (e.g. I like apples) as opposed to the specific or 'countable' plural, which is used with numbers (Bring me three apples, please). The singular for these nouns is always formed by adding the fem. sing. ending **-a** to the collective form.

collective	*singular*	*plural*	
beeḍ	béeḍa	beḍáat	*egg(s)*
bidingáan	bidingáana	bidinganáat	*aubergine(s)*
burtu'áan	burtu'áana	burtu'anáat	*orange(s)*
gamúus	gamúusa	gawamíis	*water-buffalo(es)*
Hágar	Hágara	Hagaráat	*stone(s)*
Hamáam	Hamáama	Hamamáat	*pigeon(s)*
lamúun	lamúuna	lamunáat	*lemons*
naHl	náHla	naHláat	*bee(s)*
namúus	namúusa	namusáat	*mosquito(es)*
naxl	náxla	naxláat	*palm-tree(s)*
rummáan	rummáana	rummanáat	*pomegranate(s)*
šágar	šágara	ašgáar	*tree(s)*
tuffáaH	tuffáaHa	tuffaHáat	*apple(s)*

The professions

The 'professions' are usually formed either with the Turkish ending **-gi** or on the Arabic pattern **CaCCaaC**:

agzaxáana*	→ agzági (agzagíyya)	*pharmacist, chemist*
búṣṭa*	→ buṣṭági (buṣṭagíyya)	*postman*
gázma*	→ gazmági (gazmagíyya)	*cobbler*
mákwa*	→ makwági (makwagíyya)	*one who irons laundry*
súfra*	→ sufrági (sufragíyya)	*butler*
9áraba*	→ 9arbági (9arbagíyya)	*driver of a horse and carriage*

*meaning: pharmacy, mail, shoe, iron, table-cloth, carriage.

bawwáab (bawwabíin)	*door-man*
farráaš (farrašíin)	*office-boy, attendant*
garráaH (garraHíin)	*surgeon*
naggáar (naggaríin)	*carpenter*
sawwáa' (sawwa'íin)	*driver*
ṣarráaf (ṣarrafíin)	*money changer*
šayyáal (šayyalíin)	*porter (to carry bags)*
ṭabbáax (ṭabbaxíin)	*cook*
xaddáam (xaddamíin)	*servant*
xaṭṭáaṭ (xaṭṭaṭíin)	*calligrapher*

Conditional Sentences

Arabic commonly uses three words to say 'if': **in**, **iza** and **law**. Examples:

(1)	in šaa' aḷḷáah	*God-willing*
(2)	íza 'ultílak il-Ha'íi'a Hatíz9al	*If I told you the truth, you'd get angry.*
(3)	law kunt makáanak kunt inbasáṭṭ kitíir	*If I were you, I'd be very happy.*
(4)	law Hásan ma9amálš kída ínta kunt Hatíz9al	*If Hassan had not done so, you would have gotten angry.*

There are no hard and fast rules governing the use of the three particles meaning 'if' in Colloquial Arabic (though there are in Classical Arabic), but the following may be considered general guidelines.

in : used more in expressions borrowed from Classical Arabic.

íza : usually used if the proposition stated in the 'if' clause is possible or probable; the verb following **íza** is usually perfect and the main clause verb usually imperfect.

law : usually used if the proposition stated in the 'if' clause is totally hypothetical, or at least unlikely; the verb following **law** is perfect and the main clause verb usually compound with the perfect tense of **kaan**.

III EXERCISES

Translation exercise

1. ḍarb il-Habíib zayy akl iz-zabíib [Proverb].
2. iḍ-ḍiHk min gheer sábab 'íllit ádab [Popular Saying].
3. 'wu'úu9 il-bála wála ntiẓáaruh' yá9ni wu'úu9 il-bála áHsan min intiẓáar il-bála.
4. soráyya bitHíbb is-sibáaHa wi-rukúub il-xeel.
5. iddíini tálat rummanáat min fáḍlik.
6. We ate apples and oranges.
7. Smoking is forbidden at the cinema.
8. There is no mutual understanding between the members.
9. Walking in that street is dangerous.
10. Drinking lots of wine is not good.

Additional vocabulary

Habíib	*loved one*
zabíib	*raisins*
ḍiHk	*laughing*
'íllit ádab	*lack of good manners*
wu'úu9	*falling; befalling, happening*
bála	*misfortune*
intiẓáar	*expecting*
rukúub	*riding*
xeel	*horses*
xáṭar	*danger; dangerous*

LESSON SIXTEEN
(id-dars is-siṭṭáašar)

Here are three more Goha stories.

III

márra wáaHid ídda árnab hidíyya li-gúHa. wi-ba9d usbúu9 gáluh wáaHid 9ázam náfsuh 9ánduh bi-Hígglt ínnuh ṣáaHib ṣáaHib il-árnab. gúHa 'addímluh máyya súxna 9ála innáha šúrba. fa-'álluh iṛ-ṛáagil – eeh da ya gúHa. 'álluh gúHa di šúrbit šúrbit il-árnab.

Vocabulary

ídda, yíddi	*to give*
árnab (aráanib)	*rabbit*
hidíyya (hadáaya)	*gift*
gáluh [ga + li + hu]	*came to him*
9ázam, yí9zim	*to invite*
náfsuh	*himself*
bi-Hígglt	*on the pretext*
ṣáaHib (aṣHáab)	*friend; owner*
ṣáaHib ṣáaHib il-árnab	*'a friend of the owner of the rabbit'*
'addímluh	*offered to him*
máyya súxna	*hot water*
9ála innáha	*[pretending] that it was*
šúrba	*soup*
fa	*so (an introductory particle)*

IV

sa'alu gúHa 9an ig-gawáaz 'allúhum: lá9an aḷḷáah man tazáwwag qábli wa- man tazáwwag bá9di. 'alúuluh leeh ya gúHa? 'allúhum, ílli tgáwwiz 'ábli li'ánnuh manaṣaHníiš inn il-gawáaz zift. 'alúuluh, ṭab w-ílli tgáwwiz bá9dak? 'allúhum 9alašáan ma simí9š kaláami!

Vocabulary

sá'al, yís'al (9an)	*to ask (about)*
gawáaz	*marriage*

lá9an aḷḷáah man tazáwwag qábli wa-man tazáwwag bá9di – *Goha pompously says this is Classical Arabic: 'May God curse those who [lit.: the one who] married before me and those who married after me.'*

'alúuluh	*they said to him*
li'ánnuh [li'ánna + hu]	*because he*
náṣaH, yínṣaH	*to advise*
manaṣaHníiš	*they didn't tell me [lit.: he did not advise me]*
zift	*(idiom.) terrible, awful*
ṭab = ṭáyyib	
kaláam	*talking, speaking; words*
kaláami	*that which I said*

V

wáaHid mitgáwwiz sá'al gúHa 9an rá'yuh fil-gawáaz. 'álluh gúHa inn ig-gawáaz 9áamil zayy il-birmíil ílli min foo' 9ásal wi-ba9déen tila'íih kúlluh báṣal. 'álluh iṛ-ṛáagil, waḷḷáahi, ána min sáa9it ma tgawwízt wi-kúlluh báṣal. 'álluh gúHa láazim fatáHt il-birmíil min taHt.

Vocabulary

mitgáwwiz	*married*
ra'y (aráa') fi	*opinion (on)*
barmíil (baramíil)	*barrel*
9ásal	*honey*
láa'a, yilaa'i	*to find*
kull	*all*
báṣal	*onion*
waḷḷáahi	*by God!*
min sáa9it ma	*from the moment [lit.: 'hour'] that*

tisammíiha mizaníyya tisammíiha muwázna malíiš dá9wa. ána 9áwza l-fídyu!
(*You can call it your 'budget'; you can call it 'balancing the books'; I don't care. I WANT THAT VIDEO!*)

PROVERBS

1	ig-gaar 'abl id-daar	*[Choose] the neighbour before the house*
2	iṣ-ṣabr gamíil	*Patience is beautiful, i.e. is a virtue*
3	il-'ird fi 9een úmmuh ghazáal	*A monkey, in the eye of its mother, is a gazelle*
4	mafíiš duxxáan min gheer ṇaar	*No smoke without fire*
5	ma ághla min il-wild ílla wild il-wild	*Nothing is dearer than one's children, save the children of one's children*
6	ílli ma9indúuš mayilzamúuš	*If you do not have it, you do not need it*
7	eeš yáaxud ir-riiH mil-baláaṭ	*What can the wind sweep from a tile (= you cannot have what is not there)*
8	ílli faat maat	*That which is past is dead (Don't cry over spilled milk)*
9	ibn il-wizz 9awwáam	*The gosling knows how to swim (= like father like son, in a positive sense)*
10	íkfi l-'ídra 9ála fummáha; tíṭla9 il-bint l-ummáha	*Turn the clay pot on its mouth, the daughter turns out like her mother (= like mother, like daughter)*
11	ána w-axxúuya 9ála bn 9ámmi; ána w-ibn 9ámmi 9ála l-gharíib	*My brother and I against my cousin; my cousin and I against the stranger (worth thinking about in the context of Arab politics)*

12	9ála ʾadd liHáafak midd rigléek	*Spread your quilt according to the measure of your legs (= cut your coat according to your cloth)*
13	ána báaša w-ínta báaša; miin yisuuʾ il-Humáar	*I'm a Pasha and you're a Pasha; so who drives the donkey?*
14	ḍarb il-Habíib zayy akl iz-zibíib	*A blow from your loved one is like eating raisins (i.e. something good. The loved one referred to is usually the wife)*
15	il-9een mati9láaš 9al-Háagib	*The eye does not rise above the brow (i.e. one should know one's place)*
16	il-'irš il-ábyaḍ yínfa9 fil-yoom il-íswid	*A white piastre will be useful on a black day (= a penny saved is a penny earned)*
17	in ghaab il-'uṭṭ íl9ab ya faar	*If the cat's away, go play O mouse (= . . . the mice will play)*
18	lábbis il-búuṣa tíb'a 9arúusa	*Dress up a reed and it will become a bride (like the English 'Clothes make the man' but applied to the female of the species)*
19	wáaHid šáayil dá'nuh: wit-táani za9láan leeh?	*One man is carrying his beard; so why is the other one angry (i.e. it's none of his business)*
20	umm il-9arúusa, fáḍya w-mašbúuka	*like a bride's mother: doing nothing but acting busy*
21	Habíibak yiblá9ak iz-zálaṭ; wi-9adúwwak yitmannáalak il-ghálaṭ	*Your friend will swallow stones for your sake; your enemy hopes you'll make a mistake*
22	kul ílli yi9gíbak; w-ílbis ílli yí9gib in-naas	*Eat that which pleases you; dress according to what pleases others (i.e. conform at least externally)*

23	it-ta9líim fiṣ-ṣíg̲h̲ar zayy in-na'š 9al-Hágar	*Learning in youth is like engraving in stone*
24	yí'tal il-'atíil wi-yímši fii ganáztuh	*He kills the man, then walks in his funeral (i.e. hurts s.o. then pretends to be his friend)*
25	ílli yšúfni bi-9een ašúufuh b-itnéen	*He who looks at me with one eye, I'll look at him with two (= you scratch my back, I'll scratch yours – twice as much)*
26	gíbtak ya 9abd il-mu9íin ti9ínni; la'éetak ya 9abd il-mu9íin tit9áan	*I brought you here, Abd il-Mu9iin, to help me; I found you, Abd il-Mu9iin, needing help (i.e. even more than I needed it)*
27	il-márkib ílli fiiha rayyiséen tíg̲h̲ra'	*The ship which has two captains sinks (= too many cooks spoil the broth)*
28	il-bi9íid 9an il-9een bi9íid 9an il-xáaṭir	*Literally: Out of sight, out of mind*
29	'alíil il-baxt yiláa'i il-9aḍm fil-kírša	*So unlucky that he finds bones in tripe*
30	yíddi l-Hála' l-ílli bala widáan	*He gives ear-rings to someone without ears*
31	maHáddiš wáaxid mínha Háaga	*No one takes anything from it [the world] (i.e. You can't take it with you)*
32	ḍárabu l-á9war 9ála 9éenuh; 'aal xaṣráana xasráana	*They hit the one-eyed man on his [bad] eye; he said 'what is bad is bad' (i.e. So what? Don't be concerned about what's already damaged)*
33	mala'úuš fil-ward 9eeb; 'alúuh ya áHmar il-xaddéen	*They found no fault with the roses, so they said they had red cheeks (i.e. some people will always try to find fault)*

34	il-ga9áan yíHlim bi-suu' il-9eeš	*A hungry man dreams of the bread market*
35	9umr id-damm mayíb'a máyya	*Blood will never become water (used in the sense of: Blood is thicker than water)*
36	il-maktúub 9ála l-gibíin láazim tišúufuh il-9een	*That which is written on the brow the eye must see*
37	yimúut iz-zammáar wi-ṣawáb9uh bitíl9ab	*The player dies, but his fingers keep on playing*
38	ílli íiduh fil-máyya miš zayy ílli íiduh fiṇ-ṇaar	*One whose hand is in water is not like one whose hand is in fire*
39	ílli yáakul 9ála ḍírsuh yínfa9 náfsuh	*He who chews on his own molar is self-sufficient*
40	iḍ-ḍiHk min gheer sábab 'íllit ádab	*Laughter without reason is impolite*
41	biyíHki 'íṣṣit ábu zeed	*He's telling the story of Abu Zeid (i.e. he'll go on and on talking for ages)*
42	id-dínya zayy is-sáa'iya, márra foo' wi-márra taHt	*The world is like a water-wheel; up one minute and down the next*
43	is-sirr fii biir	*The secret is in a well (i.e., you can tell me, and I won't tell anyone)*
44	báṣalit il-muHibb xarúuf	*An onion from a loved-one is like mutton*
45	wu'úu9 il-bála wi-laa ntiẓáaruh	*The actual happening of disaster is not as bad as waiting for it to happen*
46	il-aṭfáal aHbáab uḷḷáah	*Children are much loved by God*
47	ḍarábni wi-báka wi-sabá'ni w-ištáka	*He hit me and cried, then he ran off to complain before I could*

48 rabbína rabb il-'ulúub	*Our Lord is the lord of the heart: He knows our thoughts and intentions*
49 ílli yixtíši min bint 9ámmuh maygíbš mínha 9iyáal	*He who is shy with his father-in-law's daughter won't have children*
50 il-muHáami zayy il-minšáar ṭáali9 wáakil náazil wáakil	*A lawyer is like a saw; he eats when he's up, he eats when he's down (i.e. gets paid win or lose)*

READINGS

il-itnéen aHmadáat

il-itnéen aHmadáat. wáaHid 9áayiš fil-aryáaf. wit-táani 9áayiš fi maṣr. wáaHid biyištág͟hal falláaH. wit-táani biyištág͟hal ṣináa9i. wáaHid biyṭálla9 tís9a ginéeh. wit-táani itnáašar ginéeh Hásibma yíḍg͟haṭ 9ála rúuHuh fiš-šug͟hl. il-itnéen mitgawwizíin wi-mixal-lifíin. ábu Huméed ílli 9áayiš fir-riif mixállif arbá9a. wil-xáamis gayy fis-síkka. wi-ṣaHíbna lli 9áayiš fil-qaahíra mixállif itnéen wit-táalit gayy fis-síkka. ti'áabil il-awwaláani ti'últuh axbáarak eeh? yi'úllak il-Hámdu lilláah. ahé mášya. ti'últuh mášya izzáay? yi'úllak yoom 9ásal wi-yoméen báṣal. ti'últuh šidd héelak. yi'úllak iš-šidda 9al-aḷḷáah. aḷḷáah yikassíbha, id-dáaya. báṣṣit fi wišš miṛáati ba9d il-9eel it-táalit wi-'alitláha fiih fi wíššik wálad. líssa Hatgíibi wálad. kaan xállif wálad wi-bintéen. 'alitláha líssa fi wíššik wálad. Háakim id-dáaya di 9aalíma ruHíyya. fiih naas tí'ra taḍaríis il-kaff wi-nass tí'ra taḍaríis il-wišš. ṭáb9an miṛáatuh saddá'it. miš dáaya wallídit 'abl kída alf máṛṛa tíb'a 9árfa. fíḍlit tizínn 9ála dimáag͟h gúzha 9áyza kamáan wálad gamb ibnáha 9alašáan mayib'áaš li-wáHduh 9ála bintéen. ḍarúuri yigíiluh axx 9ašáan yisá9duh. fíḍlit tixállif lámma bá'u arbá9a. tálat banáat wi-wálad. wil-xáamis gayy fis-síkka. ḍarúuri il-xáamis wálad. in šaa' aḷḷáah. wi-in magáaš il-xáamis wálad wi-gat bint, yíb'a s-sáadis in šaa' aḷḷáah ḍarúuri

Hayíigi wálad. in magáaš bá'a, yíb'a ḍarúuri is-sáabi9 wálad. tífḍal is-silsílla mášya kída liHádd ma bu Huméed yíb'a dimáag͟huh tiwgá9uh. wi-bádal ma yíb'a yoom 9ásal wi-yoméen báṣal, yíb'a yoom 9ásal wi-xámsa báṣal. ábu Huméed ílli fi maṣr Haṣalítluh nafs il-Háaga. is-sitt il-Hakíima 'áalit li-mṛáatuh ba9d il-xilf it-tánya win-nábi w-ínti gáyba wálad. 'alitláha ímta? 'alitláha l-máṛṛa g-gáyya. 'alitláha išmí9na? 'alitláha 9alašáan dimáag͟h il-bint ílli xalliftíiha midawwára. law káanit miṭáwla kaanit gat ba9dáha bint. innáma madáam dimág͟hha midawwára yíb'a lli gayy waráaha wálad. garrábit wi-gáabit . . . wi-gat bint. 'áalit lil-Hakíima di gat bint. 'aalitláha mahúwwa miš min áwwil máṛṛa. min táani máṛṛa w-ismá9i kaláam. ti'áabil il-abb. izzáyyak? mayirúddiš. axbáarak eeh? lisáanuh yít'al leeh? máaši yíHsib wi-yifákkar. yigíib filúus minéen 9alašáan yíṣrif 9ála l-qabíila lli kull sána biyitzíid wáaHid. wil-miráttab kull sana mabiyizídš bi-nafs in-nísba. wil-as9áar kull sána tíṭla9 láha sillíma wálla tneen. ba9d ma kaan ábu Huméed illi hináak, w-ílli hína 9ayšíin fir-ráaHa bá'u 9ayšíin fi nakad. ba9d ma kaan il-wáaHid mínhum biyíḍHak min 'álbuh bá'a miš 9áarif Hátta šakl iḍ-ḍiHk eeh. il-9iyáal 9ayzíin sanáadil wi-hudúum wi-akl wi-dáwa wil-ginéeh ya áxxi bá'a 9áamil zayy ma yikúun sibírtu. yadúubak tiHúṭṭuh fil-gaww tibúṣṣ tila'íih itbáxxar. kull il-maṣáa9ib di gat 9alašáan kílma 'alítha id-dáaya aw il-Hakíima aw il-9ámma aw il-xáala. ḍánti líssa 9aléeki wálad, wi-wíššik wálad, dimáag͟h il-bint midawwára: yíb'a gayyílik wálad. kílma ráaHit fil-háwa kílma gáhla malaháaš má9na. bass sabbíbit mašáakil wi-humúum wi-álam. ṭuul ma l-xuráafa 9áyša f-mugtamá9na wi-bitáakul wi-bitíšrab wayyáana wi-ṭuul ma l-gahl mu9aasírna wi-9amáal yifákkar lína ṭuul ma Haníf ḍal maznu'íin. mafiiš dáwla, in-naas biyitzíid fíiha zayyína wi-tiláa'i n-naas fíiha murtáaHa. ḍarúuri tít9ab wi-tiš'a. ḍarúuri tímši tikállim nafsáha fiš-šáari9. miš kída wálla eeh?

They are both called Ahmed. One lives in the country; the other lives in Cairo. One works as a farmer; the other works as a labourer. One is paid nine pounds; the other twelve pounds working only as the spirit moves him.

Both are married and have offspring. Abu Humeed who lives in the country has had four – and the fifth is on the way. Our friend who lives in Cairo has had two – and the third is on the way.

[When] you meet the first [Ahmed and] you say to him 'What's the news?' he says to you 'Praise be to God, things are all right?' You say to him 'How all right?'; and he says 'One day of honey, two days of onion.' You say to him 'Pull yourself together,' and he says to you 'Strength [to pull oneself together] comes from God. And as for the mid-wife, may God make her prosper, she looked at my wife's face after the third child and said "In your face I see a son. You're still going to have a son".' He already had a son and two daughters, and the mid-wife says to his wife, 'You're going to have another son!'

You see, this mid-wife was a teller of fortunes. Some people read the features of the palm of the hand. Other people read the features of the face. So, of course, his wife believed [it all]. Was she not a mid-wife who had presided over births a thousand times? For sure she would know.

The wife kept on at her husband, her words ringing in his head that she wanted another son so that her first son would not be all alone with two girls. He needed a brother to come help him.

Anyway, she had another child, making four in all – three girls and a boy. Now the fifth is on the way. The fifth one for sure will be a boy . . . God willing! And if the fifth is not a boy, but a girl, then, God-willing, the sixth will surely be a boy. And if he still does not come . . . THEN THE SEVENTH WILL SURELY BE A BOY!!!

And so the chain continued like this until Abu Humeed, instead of having one day of honey and two days of onion, had for every day of honey five days of onion.

As for Abu Humeed in Cairo, the same thing happened to him. The lady doctor said to his wife after her second child, 'By the Prophet, you're going to have a son.' [The wife] asked 'When?' She said 'Next time.' [The wife] asked, 'How do you know?' She said '[I know] because the head of the girl you've just had is round. Had it been more elongated, then your next child would have been a girl. As long as the head is round like this, the next one will be a boy.'

She gave it a try, gave birth . . . and had a girl. She said to the lady-doctor, '[I had] a girl.' The doctor said to her 'It's not the first time. Next time listen to me.'

You meet the father [and ask him] 'How are you doing?' He doesn't answer. 'What's your news?' Why has the cat got his tongue? He walks around thinking and pondering. Where is he going to get the money to spend on this tribe which every year increases by one. His salary is not increasing every year at the same rate. Every year prices go up a step or two. After the Abu Humeed who is there [in the country] and the Abu Humeed who is here [in Cairo] had both been living in [relative] comfort; they are now living in hardship. Where both had used to laugh from their very hearts, they now did not know what laughter was.

The children need sandals, clothes, food and medicine. All the while the pound is like alcohol: you expose it to the air, and you see it evaporate.

All these problems stem from the fact that the midwife or the lady-doctor or a paternal aunt or a maternal aunt said something to [the wife] – 'You're going to have another son,' 'Your daughter's head is round,' 'The next one will be a boy' – words that just go into the air, ignorant words without meaning; yet they cause problems, concern and even pain. So long as superstition is alive in society, so long as it eats and drinks among us, and so long as ignorance is our contemporary and doing our thinking for us – that's how long we shall be hard-pressed. There is no country in which people increase as in ours [dramatically in number] where you find people comfortable. They can't help but be tired and suffering. They can't help walking around the streets talking to themselves. Is it not so? What do *you* think?

KEY TO EXERCISES

Lesson One

Exercise 1

Where is Muhammad?
He is in Egypt.
Where are you from?

I am from England.
Where is the book?
The book is on the table.
Is the key in the door?
No, the key is not in the door.
The key is there, beside the pen.
There is no car in front of the restaurant.

Exercise 2

1. Where is the boy?
2. He is under the bridge
3. The garden is behind the house.
4. Are there [any] books on the table?
5. Yes, there are books and a pencil on the table.
6. húmma minéen?
7. húmma min maṣr.
8. ínti gamb iš-šibbáak.
9. fiih máṭ9am fi midáan sa9d zaghlúul?
10. fiih máṭ9am hináak, wi- 'áhwa kamáan.

Lesson Two

Exercise 1

'A very short visit'
A. Hello, Samira!
B. Hello, Mahmoud.
A. How are you today?
B. Fine, thank you. And you?
A. Fine, thank you.
B. Isn't Nagwa here?
A. No, she is in Alexandria today.
B. Thank you. Good-bye.
A. Good-bye.

Exercise 2

1. Egyptians are generous.
2. The Nile is a beautiful and very long river.

3. Are the Pyramids far from here?
4. Are you Syrian or Lebanese?
5. I am neither Syrian, nor Lebanese. I'm Egyptian.
6. il-kílma sáhla.
7. fi maṣr il-maṭáa9im rixíiṣa
8. il-Harb wíHša
9. il-gúmla miš ṣá9ba.
10. iṭ-ṭarabeeza miš niḍíifa, láakin il-xaddáam miš mawgúud

Lesson Three

Exercise 1

What's your name?
My name is David Smith.
Where's your house?
My house is near Cairo Tower.

Where's the key to the office door?
The key to that door is with the doorman.

Whose is that car?
It belongs to the President of the Republic.

Cairo University is in Giza and the American University is in Liberation Square.

That case is new.
The traveller's case is new.
The case belonging to the sick traveller is on [lit. in] the plane.

Exercise 2

1. What is his name?
2. The Director's house is in Heliopolis.
3. Those farmers are tired today.
4. I have a book and a pen; but she has neither book nor pen.
5. There's your car, but where is mine?
6. béetak feen?

7. ma9indináaš beet.
8. il-gám9a di ghálya xáaliṣ.
9. il-lúkanḍa hé, láakin feen il-máṭ9am.
10. šántit il-mudíir ig-gidíida 9ind il-maṭáar.

Lesson Four

Exercise 1

1985
With us today are two good translators. The first one is from Baghdad and the other is from Damascus.
One coffee and two teas, please.
It's 5:25 a.m.
10 piasters.
55 piasters.
5 Egyptian pounds.
15 pounds sterling.
There are twelve months in a year.
Two difficult languages.

Exercise 2

1. Those five books are expensive.
2. Leila is twenty-two years old.
3. He has a lesson Monday afternoon.
4. There's a party at 7:30 pm.
5. We don't have $200 for the tickets.
6. il-xámas sitáat dool feen?
7. fiih 9išríin xaddáam fil-vílla di.
8. iṛ-ṛáagil il-Hidáašar miš mawgúud.
9. libnáan bálad ṣugháyyar láakin fíiha sítta milyóon libnáani.
10. il-9arabiyyitéen il-kubáar dool bitúu9 ra'íis il-lágna.

Lesson Five

Exercise 1

Where are you going?
I'm going to the British Embassy.

What are the children doing now?
They're sleeping.

Ali lives in Doqqi.
And where do you (f.) live?
My husband and I live in a new apartment on Hasan Sabry Street.

Who's coming from the airport today?
I (f.) really do not know.

How many new automobiles does that company want?
It wants 200.
Incredible.

Exercise 2

1. How are you going? By plane?
2. How much do they want?
3. I do not know the Ambassador's telephone number.
4. His wife is standing in the street, and her automobile is not working.
5. Mustapha is staying with us until Thursday.
6. gayyíin bil-utubíis
7. miṛáati 9áwza taláata kíilu mooz
8. mustáfa sáakin fid-dó''i wálla fig-gíiza?
9. ínta fáahim kull Háaga?
10. il-utubíis gaay bi-súr9a aw bi-šwees?

Lesson Six

Exercise 1

I'm three years older than you.
The baklava is better than the ice-cream.
Who lives in that white house?
Mounira is beautiful, but Farida is more beautiful.
The red car is newer than the green car.
Which is easier, Arabic or English?
Those two rooms are very small!

Exercise 2

1. Hassan is smaller than Raamiz.
2. That driver is blind! He is a bad driver.
3. Spring is the nicest season.
4. The apples are good, but the oranges are better.
5. Those two books are cheap.
6. ána axáff min Hásan
7. iṣ-ṣeef áHla min iš-šíta
8. il-banáat dool gumáal, láakin úxtuh ágmal
9. iskindiríyya min ágmal il-múdun il-maṣríyya
10. il-'alaméen iz-zur' dool bi-kaam.

Lesson Seven

Exercise 1

The students studied the fifth lesson the day before yesterday.
They still have not studied the sixth lesson.
What did you (pl.) do in the library?
We wrote letters to our friends in Egypt.
Did you (f.) stay at home all day?
Not at all! I went to town and ordered three silk dresses from a new shop on Suleiman Pasha St.
The workmen did not close the door when they went out.
The Arabs are famous for their poetry.
The doctor took the lift upstairs.

Exercise 2

1. Leila opened the window because inside the house there is no fresh air.
2. The children are happy because the cook has made 'mulukhiyya' again.
3. We went into the restaurant and Abdullah ordered three teas from the waiter. I didn't order anything.
4. Hassan went to Cairo with his friend.
5. Did you live in France before the war or after it.
6. daxálna l-óḍa s-sáa9a tís9a wi-nuṣṣ

7. madarástiš id-dars leeh?
8. húwwa magnúun! ḍárab 9askári wi dilwá'ti húwwa fis-sign.
9. il-mudárris bitá9na kítib maqáala 9an il-ahráam.
10. ma'a9ádiš 9ašáan húwwa mašg̲h̲úul.

Lesson Eight

Exercise 1

I understand a little French.
What will you order in the restaurant? I shall order Feta cheese, the local country bread, Fava beans and olives.
What do you and your wife study in the university, history or languages? We study neither history nor languages. I study mathematics, and my wife studies science [sciences].
Time is short. Get in the carriage and get back to the hotel.
The bill? Don't worry. You don't have to pay the bill today. You can pay tomorrow or the day after.
Please go into my office and close the drawer.
They don't know each other yet.

Exercise 2

1. I am listening to Arab music.
2. She understands Arabic well.
3. Her husband is not sitting in his office. I (f.) don't know where he is.
4. The students are doing [writing] their homework. When are you going to do your homework?
5. This is your station. Get off quickly.
6. 9áyza tišrábi eeh?
7. Hayuskúnu fi maṣr múddit tálat šuhúur.
8. miš múmkin árga9 'abl yoom il-gúm9a.
9. matḍrábiš il-wálad da! húwwa áṣg̲h̲ar mínnak.
10. híyya xáragit min šwáyya láakin Hatírga9 ba9d xámas da'áyyi'

Lesson Nine

Exercise 1

1. Visit the Sphinx.
2. She didn't bring the dessert.
3. He goes to sleep early.
4. Look over there.
5. She said so.
6. Don't go by yourself (f.)
7. You see Adel.
8. I wake up late.
9. We love Egypt.
10. Say [it]!
11. I don't forget names.
12. Answer the telephone.
13. Don't sleep (f.) on the ground.
14. I shall go to Spain.
15. He's carrying the basket.
16. We'll walk together.
17. I sold the flat.
18. I read the article.
19. I was afraid of him.
20. Run!
21. Walking
22. Putting
23. Going (pl.)
24. Fasting
25. Sleeping (f.).

Exercise 2

1. The waiter brought a cup of coffee.
2. I must see the Doctor while he's in the hospital.
3. Hussein saw that girl at the University, and after a while I saw the same girl in the restaurant.
4. Nagiib likes to sleep – he goes to bed early and wakes up late.
5. Have you answered his letter or not yet?
6. zurt il-mátHaf il-isláami wálla l-'ál9a?

7. ṣáamu fiš-šahr ramaḍáan.
8. il-falláaH šaal il-wálad lil-g̲heeṭ.
9. giib iš-šánṭa bitá9tak ma9áak.
10. 9ayzíin tirúuHu feen ba9d iḍ-ḍuhr yoom is-sabt?

Lesson Ten

1. áywa, fatáHtuh
   la, mafataHtuhúuš

2. áywa, gibnáah
   la, magibnahúuš

3. zurtúkum
   mazurtukúmš

4. áywa, ramáah
   la, maramahúuš

Lesson Eleven

Exercise 1

1. húwwa biyfákkar fi eeh?
   húmma biyfakkáru fi eeh?

2. ínta bitfáḍḍal il-bíira 9ála n-nibíit.
   íHna binfáḍḍal il-bíira 9ála n-nibíit.

3. láazim tig̲háyyir hudúmha bi-súr9a.
   láazim tig̲hayyíru hudúmkum bi-súr9a.

4. wálduh sáafir aswáan . . . .
   agdáaduh sáfru aswáan . . . .

5. Hásan biydárris 9árabi wálla nglíizi?
   nádya wi-Hásan biydarrísu . . . .?

Exercise 2

1. il-fallaHíin Háwlu yimawwítu l-Háyya.

2. il-mudarrisíin biyfahhímu ṭ-ṭulláab id-dars.

3. iṭ-ṭabbaxíin biyHaḍḍáru l-9áša

4. il-9ummáal dool miš Hayiḍríbu.

Lesson Twelve

I

Once Goha was sitting under a hazel-nut tree, and he began to wonder why God [lit. = in what the wisdom that our Lord . . .] let a big tree give forth small nuts while He let the watermelon, so much bigger than a hazel-nut, have a small branch which cannot carry it. From so much thinking Goha fell asleep. Then he suddenly awoke startled by a hazel-nut which had fallen on his head. He said: 'Praise be to God. My Lord I have understood Your wisdom that this big tree doesn't give forth watermelon. [Had it done so, that] would have been the end of me!'

II

Once Goha was walking along and children began to tease him. In order to get rid of them he told them that there was a party at the house of his friend, Hagg 9ali. The children believed him and ran off as fast as they could [lit. = their tails in their teeth]. After they had gone, Goha thought that perhaps there really was a party, and off he ran [he too] to the house of Hagg 9ali.

Lesson Thirteen

Exercise 1

1. We must learn French.
2. Where will you meet?

3. She graduated last year.
4. It's possible that I may be a bit late.
5. Our friends enjoyed themselves a lot.
6. Speak with him.
7. Don't (pl.) be late!
8. The door opened.
9. He and I must understand one another.
10. The mirror has broken.

Exercise 2

1. húda dáyman bitit'áxxar
   húmma dáyman biyit'axxáru

2. ínti Hatitxarrági min ig-gám9a . . .
   húwwa Hayitxárrag . . . .

3. íHna láazim nit'áabil . . . .
   íntu láazim tit'áblu . . . .

4. húmma biyHíbbu yit9áššu . . . .
   nabíila bitHíbb tit9áášša . . . .

5. iṭ-ṭaalíba l-ingiliizíyya di gat maṣr 9ašáan tit9állim 9árabi
   iṭ-ṭulláab il-ingilíiz dool gum maṣr 9ašáan yit9allímu 9árabi

Lesson Fourteen

Exercise 1

1. My father works as a journalist.
2. What will you buy in Khan al-Khalili.
3. Leila got sun-burned.
4. We must ask to be excused now.
5. Hassan bought a new bicycle.
6. May I use your dictionary.
7. All the pedestrians are in a hurry.

Exercise 2

1. húwwa biyištághal muHáami
   ínta bitištághal muHáami

2. il-mudarrísa Hatista'íil búkra
   a9ḍáa' il-máglis Hayista'íilu búkra

3. híyya istálamit il-filúus min il-bank
   húmma istálamu l-filúus min il-bank

4. ána ištaréet tázkara lil-masraHíyya
   miṛáati ištárit . . . .

5. iš-šuyúux muHtaramíin
   ra'íisit il-wúzara muHtárama

Lesson Fifteen

1. Being hit by one's beloved is like eating raisins.
2. Laughing without reason is rude.
3. 'wu'úu9 il-bála wála ntiẓáaruh' means that the happening of misfortune is better than expecting misfortune [to happen].
4. Thoraya likes swimming and horseback riding.
5. Give me three pomegranates please.
6. kálna tuffáaH wi-burtu'áan.
7. it-tadxíin mamnúu9 fis-sínima.
8. mafíiš tafáahum been il-a9ḍáa'.
9. il-mášy fiš-šáari9 da xáṭar.
10. šurb nibíit kitíir miš kwáyyis.

Lesson Sixteen

III

Once someone gave a rabbit as a present to Goha. A week later someone invited himself to his house on the pretext that he was a friend of the owner of the rabbit [ṣáaHib ṣáaHib il-árnab]. Goha offered him hot water [saying] that it was soup. The man said to him, 'what's this, Goha?' Goha said to him, that is soup of the soup of the rabbit [šúrbit šúrbit il-árnab]!

IV

They asked Goha about marriage. He said to them: 'May God curse those who married before me and those married after me.'

'Why, Goha?'

'Those who married before me because they did not advise me that marriage was so awful.'

'Well, and those who married after you?'

'Because they didn't listen to what I said!'

V

One who was married asked Goha for his opinion on marriage. Goha said to him: 'Marriage is like a barrel which has honey in the top, and then underneath you find nothing but onion.'

The man said to him: 'I swear, from the moment I married it's been all onion.'

Goha replied: 'You should have opened the barrel from underneath!'

ARABIC–ENGLISH GLOSSARY

a

’áabil, yi’áabil to meet (*trans.*)
’aal, yi’úul to say
’aam, yi’úum to get up; wake up
aanísa (anisáat) Miss
’aas, yi’íis to measure; try on
áaxir last
áaya (ayáat) Koranic or Biblical verse
’áa9id, ’á9da, ’a9díin sit(ting); stay(ing)
’ábaḍ, yí’baḍ to get paid
’ábaḍ, yú’buḍ to arrest
ábadan never; ever; not at all
abažúura (abažuráat) lamp(shade)
abb (abbaháat) father
’ábbaḍ, yi’ábbaḍ to pay (wages)
’abl before
’abl ma + *vb.* before
abríil April
abríi’ (abaríi’) pitcher
abu galámbu crab
ábu l-hool Sphinx
ábyaḍ, béeḍa, biiḍ white
ádab (adáab) literature, belles lettres; manners
’ádam (i’dáam) foot
’add extent
’áḍḍa, yi’áḍḍi to spend (time)
’áddim, yi’áddim to present, put forward
’adíim, ’adíima, ’udáam old, ancient
’áfal, yí’fil to close
afrángi, afrangíyya, afráng foreign, ‘western’
agáaza (agazáat) holiday, vacation
águar, yi’águar to rent
agzági (agzagíyya) pharmacist
agzaxáana (agzaxanáat) pharmacy
ag̲h̲labíyya majority

agh̲úsṭus August
'áhwa coffee; café
áHmar, Hámra, Humr red
áHrag, yíHrig to embarrass
aHyáanan sometimes
akl food
ákram, yíkrim to be hospitable to
'ála, yí'li to fry
'álam (a'láam) pen
'ála9, yí'la9 to undress, take off
alf (aláaf) thousand
'all, yi'íll to decrease
aḷḷáah God
almáani, almaníyya, almáan German
'ál9a citadel
ámal (amáal) hope
'ámar moon
amíir (úmara) prince
'amH wheat
'amíiṣ ('umṣáan) shirt
ámma but; as for
ámmin, yi'ámmin to insure
amr (awáamir) order
amrikáani, amrikaníyya, amrikáan American
ámṭar, tímṭir to rain
ána I
anáani, ananíyya, ananiyyíin selfish
anf (unúuf) nose
'ára, yí'ra to read
'áraṣ, yú'ruṣ to sting (e.g. insects); to pinch
arbá9a four
arba9ṭáašar fourteen
'aríib ('aráayib) relative
arbi9íin forty
arḍ (aráaḍi) land, ground; floor
árnab (aráanib) rabbit
'árrab, yi'árrab to draw near; be about to
ásad (usúud) lion
ásar (asáar) ancient ruins
ásbat, yísbit to prove

áslam, yíslam to become a Moslem
aswáan Aswan
'aṣd intent
'aṣr ('uṣúur) palace
aṣanṣéer (aṣanṣeráat) lift, elevator
ásfar, ṣáfra, ṣufr yellow
aṣl (uṣúul) origin
aṣli, aṣlíyya, aṣliyyíin original
'aṣṣ, yi'úṣṣ to cut (e.g. with scissors)
'átal, yí'til to kill
'áṭa9, yí'ṭa9 to cut; buy a ticket
'aṭr ('uṭuráat) train
áṭraš, ṭárša, ṭurš deaf
'áṭṭa9, yi'áṭṭa9 to cut (into many pieces)
áxḍar, xáḍra, xuḍr green
axíir, axíira, axiríin last; latest
axíiran finally, at last
axráani, axraníyya, axraniyyíin last
áxras, xársa, xurs dumb, mute
áxxar, yi'áxxar to delay
aw or
'áwi very
awwaláani, awwalaníyya, awwalaniyyíin first
áwwil ma + *v.* as soon as
áwwil, úula, awáa'il first
'áwwim, yi'áwwim to cause to get up
áyḍan also
áywa yes
ayy which?; any
áẓhar, yíẓhir to show
ázra', zár'a, zur' blue
'á9ad, yú'9ud to sit down; stay
á9ma, 9ámya, 9umy blind
á9rag, 9árga, 9urg lame
á9war, 9óora, 9uur one-eyed

b

baab (abwáab) door
baal thought, care

báaligh, yibáaligh to exaggerate
baar (baráat) bar
báarik, yibáarik to bless
báas, yibúus to kiss
báaša, bašawáat pasha
baat, yibáat to stay overnight
baaṭ (baṭáat) armpit
báayix, báyxa, bayxíin unpleasant
baaẓ, yibúuẓ to become damaged, spoiled
baa9, yibíi9 to sell
báa'i, bá'ya, ba'yíin remaining
báa'i (small) change
bádal min instead of
bádawi, badawíyya, bádu Bedouin
bádla (bídal) suit (of clothes)
bádri early
báHas, yíbHas to investigate; do research
baHHáar (baHHáara) sailor
baHr (biHáar) sea
baHs research, inquiry
báka, yíbki to weep, cry
baláaš Never mind!
baláaṭ (*c.*), **baláaṭa** (*s.*), **(balaṭáat)** tile(s)
bálad (*f.*), **(biláad)** country; town
báladi, baladíyya, baladiyyíin local, native
baladíyya municipality
bálaH (*c.*) dates
bálṭu (baláaṭi) overcoat
bámya okra
banafsígi purple
bank (bunúuk) bank
bansyóon (bansyonaat) 'pension', boarding-house
banṭalóon (banṭalonáat) trousers
báraka (barakáat) blessing
bára, yíbri to sharpen
bára', yúbru' to glitter
bard cold
bardáan, bardáana, bardaníin cold
bárḍu also

baríid post, mail
barmíil (baramíil) barrel
barr land (opposite of 'sea')
bárra outside
basíiṭ, basíiṭa, busáaṭ small; trifling
bass only, just
báṣal (*c.*), **báṣala** (*s.*), **(baṣaláat)** onion
baṣṣ, yibúṣṣ to look
baṭáaṭiṣ (*c.*) potatoes
baṭn (*f.*), **(buṭúun)** stomach
baṭṭáal, baṭṭáala, baṭṭalíin bad; unemployed
báṭṭal, yibáṭṭal to stop, put a stop to (a habit)
baṭṭaníyya (battaniyyáat) blanket
baṭṭíix (*c.*), **baṭṭíixa** (*s.*), **(baṭṭixáat)** watermelon
bawwáab (bawwabíin) doorman
báwwaẓ, yibáwwaẓ to damage, spoil (*trans.*)
baxíil, baxíila, búxala miser(ly)
baxt luck
bayyáa9 (bayya9íin) seller
báyyaḍ, yibáyyaḍ to whitewash
bá9at, yíb9at to send
ba9d after
ba9d ma + *v.* after
ba9déen afterwards, later
ba9ḍ some; each other
bá'a then, well
bá'a, yíb'a to become
ba'dúunis parsley
ba'láawa baklava
ba'šíiš baksheesh
ba'' (*c.*), **ba''áaya** (*s.*), **(ba''áat)** bugs
ba''áal (ba''alíin) grocer
beeḍ (*c*), **béeḍa** (*s.*), **(beḍáat)** eggs
been between
beet (buyúut) house
bee9 (*v.n.*) selling, sale
benzíin petrol, gasoline
bi by, with
bidingáan (*c.*), **bidingáana** (*s.*), **(bidinganáat)** eggplant

bidúun without
biḍáa9a (baḍáayi9) merchandise, goods
bihíima (baháayim) beast (of burden)
bíiba (bibáat) pipe (for smoking)
biir (abáar) well
bíira beer
bináaya (binayáat) building
bint (banáat) girl, daughter
birnáamig (baráamig) programme, course
bisílla (*c.*) peas
bišwéeš slowly
bitáa9, bitá9t, bitúu9 of, belonging to
bitíllu veal
bitróol petroleum
bi9íid, bi9íida, bu9áad far, distant
borg (burúug) tower
buHáyra (buHayráat) lake
búkra tomorrow
bulíis police
búndu' (*c.*), **búndu'a** (*s.*), **(bundu'áat)** hazel-nuts
bunn coffee
búnni brown
burtu'áan (*c.*), **burtu'áana** (*s.*), **(burtu'anáat)** oranges
burtu'áani orange (colour)
búṣṭa post
buṣṭági (buṣṭagíyya) postman
butagáaz Butagaz
buur sa9íid Port Said
búuya (buyáat) paint
buxáar steam
bu9d distance
bu'' mouth

d

da, di, dool this, that, these, those
daar (duur) house
daas, yidúus (9ála) to step on
dáawa, yidáawi to treat (medically)

daax, yidúux to get dizzy
dáaxil inside
dáayi', yidáayi' to annoy, bother
daa', yidúu' to taste (food)
dábaH, yídbaH to slaughter (by cutting the throat)
dáfa9, yídfa9 to push; pay
daf9 (v.n.) paying; payment
dáhab gold
dáhan, yídhin to paint
dall, yidúll to indicate
dálla9, yidálla9 to spoil, be too nice to
damm blood
dáraga (daragáat) degree, class
dáras, yídris to study
dárris, yidárris to teach
dars (durúus) lesson
dáwa (m.), (adwíya) medicine
dáwla (dúwal) nation
dáwša commotion, noise
dáwwar, yidáwwar (9ala) to look for
dáwwa', yidáwwa' to let s.o. taste
dáxal, yúdxul to enter
dáyman always
dáyya', dayyá'a, dayya'íin narrow
dáyya', yidáyya' to make tight
da'n (f.), (du'úun) chin; beard
da'', yidú'' to knock, ring
dibbáan (*c.*), **dibbáana** (*s.*), **(dibbanáat)** flies
diib (diyáaba) wolf
diik rúumi turkey
diin (adyáan) religion
díini, diníyya, diniyyíin religious
dilwá'ti now
dimáagh brain
dínya world
diráasa (dirasáat) study
diráa9 (adrí9a) arm
disímbir December
di'íi'a (da'áayi') minute

dubáara string
dúghri straight
duktóor (dakátra) doctor
duláab (dawalíib) cupboard
durg (adráag) drawer
duxúul (*v.n.*) entering
duxxáan smoke

ḍ

ḍáani mutton
ḍaa9, yiḍíi9 to be lost
ḍáffa (ḍifáaf) river-bank
ḍahr (ḍuhúur) back
ḍaláam darkness
ḍálma darkness
ḍamíir (ḍamáayir) conscience
ḍárab, yíḍrab to beat, hit
ḍarb (*v.n.*) hitting
ḍárba (ḍarbáat) blow
ḍarúuri, ḍaruríyya, ḍaruriyyíin necessary; essential
ḍáyya9, yiḍáyya9 to lose
ḍeef (ḍuyúuf) guest
ḍidd against
ḍíHik, yíḍHak to laugh
ḍiHk (*v.n.*) laughing
ḍoo' light
ḍuhr noon

e

eeh what?

f

faad, yifíid to benefit (trans.)
fáaḍi, fáḍya, faḍyíin empty; unoccupied
fáaḍil, fáḍla, faḍlíin remain(ing)
fáahim, fáhma, fahmíin understand(ing)

fáakir, fákra, fakríin remember(ing)
faar (firáan) mouse
fáarigh, fárgha, farghíin empty
fáaṣil, yifáaṣil to bargain
faat, yifúut to pass
faddáan (fadadíin) feddan
fáḍḍa silver
faḍḍal, yifáḍḍal to prefer
fáhhim, yifáhhim to explain, cause to understand
fáHaṣ, yífHaṣ to examine
faHm (*c.*) coal
fakaháani (fakahaníyya) fruit vendor
fákha (fawáakih) fruit
fakk jaw
fakk, yifúkk to untie; to get change (money)
fákka (small) change
fákkar, yifákkar to think; remind
falláaH, falláaHa, fallaHíin farmer, peasant
fállis, yifállis to be broke, bankrupt
falsáfa philosophy
fann (funúun) art
fannáan, fannáana, fannaníin artist
fánni, fanníyya, fanniyyíin technical
fáram, yúfrum to grind
faránsa France
faransáawi, faransawíyya, faransawiyyíin French
fáraš, yífriš to spread (e.g. a cloth); furnish
faráwla (*c.*) strawberries
farHáan, farHáana, farHaníin happy
farráaš (farrašíin) office tea-boy and messenger
fárrag, yifárrag to show
fárraH, yifárraH to make joyful
farš furniture
fárxa (firáax) chicken
far9 (furúu9) branch
far9óoni, far9oníyya, faráa9na Pharaonic
far' (furúu') difference
fássaH, yifássaH to take on an outing
fássar, yifássar to explain

faṣl (fuṣúul) season; classroom
faṣúlya (*c.*) (green) beans
faššáar (faššaríin) braggart
fataH, yíftaH to open
fátaš, yíftiš (is-sirr) to disclose (secret)
fáttaH, yifáttaH to open eyes
fattáaHa (fattaHáat) opener
fatúura (fawatíir) bill
fáwwit, yifáwwit to cause to pass
fazzúura (fawazíir) riddle
fa'íir, fa'íira, fú'ara poor
feen where?
fi in
fibráayir February
fíḍil, yífḍal to remain, continue
fíḍi, yífḍa to become empty, unoccupied
figl (*c.*), **fígla** (*s.*), **(figláat)** radish
fíhim, yífham to understand
fiih there is/are
fíkra (afkáar) idea
fílfil (*c.*) pepper
filistíin Palestine
filúus (*f.*) money
fingáan (fanagíin) cup
fíriH, yífraH to feel joyful
fiṣáal (*v.n.*) bargaining
fíṭir, yífṭar to eat breakfast, eat s.th. for breakfast
fi9l (af9áal) verb
foo' over; above
fukáaha humour
fulúuka (faláayik) fellucca (sailing boat)
furn (afráan) oven
fúrṣa (fúraṣ) opportunity; occasion
fúrša (fúraš) brush
fúsHa excursion, outing
fustáan (fasatíin) dress
fuṭúur breakfast
fuul sudáani (*c.*) peanuts
fuul (*c.*) fava (broad) beans
fúuṭa (fúwaṭ) towel; napkin

g

gaab, yigíib to bring
gáahiz, gáhza, gahzíin ready
gáami9 (gawáami9) mosque
gaar (giráan) neighbour
gáawib, yigáawib to answer
gáayiz it's possible
gaay, gáaya, gayíin come (coming)
gaaz kerosine
gaa9, yigúu9 to become hungry
gabáan, gabáana, gúbana coward(ly)
gábal (gibáal) mountain
gáhhiz, yigáhhiz to prepare
gah, yíigi to come
gállid, yigállid to bind (books)
gamáal beauty
gámal (gimáal) camel
gáma9, yígma9 to collect, add
gamb beside
gambári (*c.*) shrimp, prawn
gamíil, gamíila, gumáal beautiful
gamíi9 all
gamúus (*c.*), **gamúusa** (*s.*), **(gawamíis)** water buffalo
gam9 plural
gám9a (gam9áat) university
gánna paradise
gánnin, yigánnin to drive mad
ganúub south
garáaž (garažáat) garage
gáras (agráas) bell
gára, yígra to happen
garíida (garáayid) newspaper
garráaH (garaHíin) surgeon
garr, yigúrr to drag
garsóon (garsonáat) waiter
gatóoh cake
gawáab (gawabáat) letter
gaww weather
gayy (= gaay) come (coming)

gázar (*c.*) carrots
gázma (gízam) shoe
gazmágí (gazmagíyya) cobbler
gazzáar (gazzaríin) butcher
ga9áan, ga9áana, ga9aníin hungry
gíbna cheese
gidd (gudúud) grandfather
gídda (giddáat) grandmother
gíddan very
gidíid, gidíida, gudáad new
gild skin; leather
ginéeh (gineháat) pound, £
ginéena (ganáayin) garden
gíri, yígri to run
gism (agsáam) body
gooz (agwáaz) husband
gumhuríyya (gumhuriyyáat) republic
gúmla (gúmal) sentence
gúmruk (gamáarik) Customs
gurnáan (garaníin) newspaper
gúwwa in(side)
gu9ráan (ga9aríin) scarab

gh

ghaab, yighíib to be absent
gháali, ghálya, ghalyíin expensive
ghaar, yighíir (min) to be jealous of; (9ála) be jealously protective of
ghxuáayib, gháyba, ghaybíin absent
ghaaz gas
ghaaz, yighíiz to tease; make angry
gháda (*m.*) lunch
ghádda, yigháddi to give lunch
ghálab, yíghlab to beat (in a game)
ghála, yíghli to boil (*intr.*)
ghálṭa (ghálaṭ) mistake, error
ghalṭáan, ghalṭáana, ghalṭaníin mistaken; at fault
ghámmaḍ, yighámmaḍ to close (eyes)

ghání, ghaníyya, ághniya rich
ghánna, yighánni) to sing
gháraḍ (aghráaḍ) object, purpose
gharb west
ghárbi, gharbíyya, gharbiyyíin western(er)
gharíib, gharíiba, ghúraba strange(r)
ghásal, yíghsil to wash
ghašš, yighíšš to cheat, swindle
ghaššáaš, ghaššáaša, ghaššašíin cheater
gháṭa (ghutyáan) cover
gháyyar, yigháyyar to change
ghazáal (ghizláan) gazelle
ghíliṭ, yíghlaṭ to make a mistake
ghíli, yíghla to become expensive
ghíri', yíghra' to drown (intr.)
ghubáar dust
ghuráab (ghirbáan) crow

h

háadi, hádya, hadyíin calm
haat, háati, háatu bring!
háayil, háyla, haylíin superb
hábaš, yíhbiš to snatch
hamm, yihímm to concern
handása engineering; geometry
háram (ahráam) pyramid
háwa (*m.*) air
háwwa, yiháwwi to ventilate
házzar, yiházzar (má9a) to joke with
hidíyya (hadáaya) gift
hiláal crescent
hína here
hináak there
híndi, hindíyya, hunúud Indian
hiwáaya (hiwayáat) hobby
híyya she
hudúum clothes

húmma they
húwwa he

H

Háaḍir, Háḍra, Haḍríin present; 'yes, certainly'
Háafi, Háfya, Hafyíin barefoot
Háaga (Hagáat) thing; something
Haal (aHwáal) condition, state
Háalan at once
Háasib, yiHáasib to add up; settle accounts with
Háawil, yiHáawil to try
Habb, yiHíbb to like; love
Habíib, Habíiba, Habáayib dear, beloved
Hadd someone
Hadd (Hudúud) border, frontier; limit
Hadíid iron (metal)
Hadíis, Hadíisa, Hudáas modern
Hádsa (Hawáadis) accident
Haḍáana kindergarten
Haḍáara, Haḍaráat civilization
Háḍḍar, yiHáḍḍar to prepare
Haḍrít(ak, etc.) you (formal)
Háfar, yúHfur to dig; drill
Háfla (Hafaláat) party (celebration)
Hágar (*c.*), **Hágara** (*s.*), **(Hagaráat)** stone
Hágaz, yíHgiz to reserve, book
Hagg, yiHígg to go on pilgrimage
Háka, yíHki to relate (a story)
Haláal (religiously) allowed
Haláawa (Halawiyyáat) dessert, sweet
Hálam, yíHlam to dream
Hála' (Hil'áan) ear-ring
Hála', yíHla' to shave
Hálla (Hílal) (cooking) pot
Hálla, yiHálli to eat dessert, (s.th) for dessert
Hall, yiHíll to solve
Hamáam (*c.*), **Hamáama** (*s.*), **(Hamamáat)** pigeon
Hamd praise (of God)

Hammáam (Hammamaat) bath(room)
Hámmil, yiHámmil to load
Hanafíyya (Hanafiyyáat) tap, faucet
Hanṭúur (Hanaṭíir) gharry, carriage
Haráam (religiously) forbidden
Haráami (Haramíyya) thief
Haráara temperature; heat
Hára', yíHra' to burn
Harb (Hurúub) war
Harf (Hurúuf) letter (of alphabet)
Haríir silk
Haríi' fire (out of control)
Harr heat
Harráan, Harráana, Harraníin hot
Hásab, yíHsib to count
Hass, yiHíss to feel
Háṣal, yíHṣal to happen
Háṣba measles
Hášara (Hašaráat) insect
Háša, yíHši to stuff (food)
Hašíiš grass; hashish
Haššáaš (Haššašíin) hashish addict
Haṭṭ, yiHúṭṭ to put
Hawáali approximately
Háwwal, yiHáwwal to transform
Háwwiš, yiHáwwiš to save, hoard
Hayáah (*f.*) life
Hayawáan (Hayawanáat) animal
Hayy (aHyáa') neighbourhood, quarter
Haẓẓ luck, good fortune
Ha'íi'a (Ha'áayi') fact
Ha'l (Hu'úul) field
Ha'' (Hu'úu') right(s)
Heeṭ (Heṭáan) wall
Hibr ink
Hidáašar eleven
Hiddáaya (Hiddayáat) kite (bird)
Híḍir, yíHdar to attend
Hífiẓ, yíHfaẓ to memorize

Higg pilgrimage
Híila (Híyal) trick
Hikáaya (Hikayáat) story
Híkma (Híkam) maxim; wisdom
Hílif, yíHlif to swear (e.g., on one's honour)
Hilm (aHláam) dream
Hilw, Hílwa, Hilwíin pretty, nice
Hisáab bill; arithmetic
Ḥiṭṭa (Ḥiṭaṭ) bit, piece; place
Hizáam (Hízima) belt
Hizb (aHzáab) (political) party
Hooš (aHwáaš) courtyard
Hubb love
Hukm judgement
Hukúuma (Hukumáat) government
Hukúumi, Hukumíyya, Hukumiyyíin governmental
Humáar (Himíir) donkey, ass
Hurríyya freedom
Hurr, Húrra, aHráar free (e.g. politically)
Huṣáan (Híṣina) horse
Husúul (*v.n.*) happening

i

'íbil, yí'bal to accept
iblíis Satan, the devil
ibn son
ibtáda, yibtídi to begin
'íbṭi, 'ibṭíyya, a'báaṭ Copt, Coptic
ibtidáa'i, ibtida'íyya, ibtida'iyyíin primary, beginning (*adj.*)
iddáayi', yiddáayi' to get upset
ídda, yíddi to give
'ídim, yí'dam to become ancient
'ídir, yí'dar to be able
iḍráab (iḍrabáat) strike (political)
iftákar, yiftíkir to think
igáar (igaráat) rent
igtimáa9i, igtima9íyya, igtima9iyyíin social
ihtámm, yihtámm (bi) to be interested in

iHmárr, yiHmárr to be(come) red; get sun-burn
íHna we
iHtáag, yiHtáag to need
iHtáram, yiHtírim to respect
iid (idéen) hand
ílla minus; except
ílli that, which, who
imáan faith
imbáariH yesterday
ímta when?
imtiHáan (imtiHanáat) exam
in if
inbásaṭ, yinbísiṭ to be happy
ingíil Bible
ingiltíra England
ingilíizi, ingilizíyya, ingilíiz English
inkásar, yinkísir to break (intrans.)
inn that
innahárda today
insáan human being, Man
ínta you (*m.*)
intáag production
ínti you (*f.*)
íntu you (*pl.*)
iqtiṣáad economics
iqtiṣáadi, iqtiṣadíyya, iqtiṣadiyyíin economic
'irš ('urúuš) piastre
isháal diarrhoea
iskindiríyya Alexandria
isláam Islam
isláami, islamíyya, islamiyyíin Islamic
ism (asáami) name
isra'íil Israel
isra'íili, isra'ilíyya, isra'iliyyíin Israeli
istágh̲rab, yistágh̲rab to be surprised
istálaf, yistílif to borrow
istálam, yistílim to receive
istánna, yistánna to wait
istaráyyaH, yistaráyyaH to rest

istá9gil, yistá9gil to hurry
istá9mil, yistá9mil to use
ista'áal, yista'íil to resign
istá'zin, yistá'zin to excuse o.s.; ask permission
istimáara (istimaráat) form (to fill out)
istiwáana (istawanáat) record
isti'áala (isti'aláat) resignation
isti'láal independence
íswid, sóoda, suud black
iswíra (asáawir) bracelet
išáara (išaráat) sign, signal
išráaf supervision
istághal, yistághal to work (as)
ištára, yištíri to buy
'íšṭa cream
itfárrag, yitfárrag (9ala) to have a look at, look around, watch
itgáddid, yitgáddid to be renewed
itgáwwiz, yitgáwwiz to get married
itghádda, yitghádda to eat lunch, eat for lunch
itHássin, yitHássin to improve
itháyya', yitháyya' (li, lu) to seem, appear
itkállim, yitkállim (má9a) to speak
itmárran, yitmárran to practice
itnáašar twelve
itnéen two
ittáfa', yittífi' to agree
ittiHáad (ittiHadáat) union
it9állim, yit9állim to learn
it9ášša, yit9ášša to have dinner
it'ággil, yit'ággil to be postponed
it'áxxar, yit'áxxar to be late
iṭálya Italy
ixtáar, yixtáar to choose
íza if
izáa9a broadcasting
izzáay how?
i9dáadi, i9dadíyya, i9dadiyyíin preparatory (e.g. school)
i9láan (i9lanáat) advertisement

k

kaam how many?; a few
káamil, kámla, kamlíin complete, perfect
kaan, yikúun to be
káatib (kuttáab) writer; clerk
kábbar, yikábbar to enlarge
kabb, yikúbb to pour, spill
kabríit matches
kaddáab, kaddáaba, kaddabíin liar
káffa, yikáffi to be enough
kaHH, yikúHH to cough
kahrába electricity
kahramáan amber
kaláam talk
kalb (kiláab) dog
kállif, yikállif to cost
kállim, yikállim to speak to
kal, yaákul to eat
kamáan also
kamaliyyaat luxuries
kámira (kamiráat) camera
kámmil, yikámmil to complete, continue
kánaba (kánab) sofa, couch
kánaka (kanakáat) Arabic coffee pot
kánas, yíknis to sweep
karíim, karíima, kúrama generous
karkadéeh hibiscus
kásar, yíksar to break
kasláan, kasláana, kaslaníin lazy
kássil, yikássil to feel lazy
kásaf, yíksif to embarrass
kátab, yíktib to write
káwa, yíkwi to iron
káwkab (kawáakib) planet
káwwan, yikáwwan to form (*trans.*)
kazíno (kazinoháat) 'casino' = open-air restaurant
kazzáab, kazzáaba, kazzabíin liar

kíbda liver
kibíir, kibíira, kubáar big; large
kíbir, yíkbar to become large, grow
kída so, thus
kídib, yíkdib (9ála) to lie (to)
kifáaya enough
kíilo kilogram
kiis (akyáas) bag (paper or plastic)
kílma (kilmáat) word
kilomítr kilometer
kílwa (kaláawi) kidney
kiníisa (kanáayis) church
kísib, yíksab to win; gain, profit
kitáaba (*v.n.*) writing
kitáab (kútub) book
kitíir, kitíira, kutáar many, much; a lot
kízib, yíkzib (9ála) to lie (to)
kóora (kúwar) ball
kóosa (*c.*) squash
korníiš 'Corniche'
kubbáaya (kubbayáat) drinking glass
kúbri (kabáari) bridge
kull every, all; each
kullíyya (kulliyyáat) college
kummítra (*c.*) pear
kumsáari (kumsaríyya) ticket collector (on bus, train, etc.)
kuṛṛáasa (kaṛaṛíis) notebook
kúrsi (karáasi) chair
kurúmb (*c.*) cabbage
kuttáab (katatíib) village school
kwáyyis, kwayyísa, kwayyisíin good

l

laa no
láabis, lábsa, labsíin wear(ing)
láaHiẓ, yiláaHiẓ to observe
láakin but
láa9ib, yiláa9ib to play with s.o.; player

láa'a, yiláa'i to find; to meet (s.o.)
lában milk
lábbis, yilábbis to dress s.o.
laff, yilíff to turn; wrap; take a walk
lágha, yílghi to cancel
láhga (lahgáat) dialect
láHma meat
lámma when
lamúun (*c.*), **lamúuna** (*s.*), **lamunáat** lemon
lándan London
laṭíif, laṭíifa, luṭáaf nice (of a person)
law if
láxbaṭ, yiláxbaṭ to muddle, confuse
lazíiz, lazíiza, luzáaz delicious
la' no
leeh why?
leel night(time)
léela (layáali) night
li for; to
líbis, yílbis to get dressed, put on
líbya Libya
ligháayit until
liHáaf quilt
líssa not yet; still
lí9ib, yíl9ab to play
li'ánn because
loon (alwáan) colour
looz (*c.*) almonds
lubnáan Lebanon
lubnáani, lubnaníyya, lubnaniyyíin Lebanese
lúgha (lugháat) language
lukánḍa (lukanḍáat) hotel
lú'sur Luxor

m

máaḍi, máḍya, maḍyíin past
maal (amwáal) wealth, funds, money
máani9 objection

máaris March
máaši okay, all right
máaši, mášya, mašyíin walk(ing)
maat, yimúut to die
máayu May
máblagh (mabáaligh) amount
mabrúuk congratulations!
mabsúuṭ, mabsúuṭa, mabsuṭíin happy, glad
madd, yimídd to stretch, extend
madíina (múdun) city; Medina
madrása (madáaris) school
máḍa, yímḍi to sign
mafhúum understood
mafrúuḍ supposed (to)
mafrúuš, mafrúuša, mafrušíin furnished
magálla (magalláat) magazine
mághrib sunset, evening
máglis (magáalis) place of gathering and assembly
magnúun, magnúuna, maganíin crazy, mad
maHáll (maHalláat) place
maHáṭṭa (maHaṭṭáat) station
maHdúud, maHdúuda, maHdudíin limited
maHfáẓa (maHáafiẓ) wallet
makáan (amáakin) place
makaróona macaroni
mákka Mecca
maknása (makáanis) broom
máktab (makáatib) office, desk
maktába (makáatib) library; bookstore
mákwa (makáawi) iron
makwági (makwagíyya) one who irons
mála, yímla to fill
malH salt
málik (mulúuk) king
málika (malikáat) queen
mallíim (malalíim) milleme
malyáan, malyáana, malyaníin full
mamnúun, mamnúuna, mamnuníin grateful
mána9, yímna9 to prevent; forbid

mandíil (manadíil) handkerchief
mánga (*c.*), **mangáaya** (*s.*), **(mangáat)** mango
manṭí'a (manáati') area, zone
mánẓar (manáaẓir) view, sight
máṛa woman, wife (cf. **miṛáatu)**
máṛaḍ (amṛáaḍ) disease
marHála (maráaHil) phase, stage
maríiḍ, maríiḍa, marḍa sick, ill
márkaz (maráakiz) position; centre; station
márkib (*f.*), **(maráakib)** ship
máṛṛa (maṛṛáat) time(s)
marr, yimúrr to pass
marwáHa (maráawiH) fan
masáafa (masafáat) distance
másaH, yímsaH to wipe
másal (amsáal) proverb, saying
másalan for example
másgid (masáagid) mosque
masíiHi, masiHíyya, masiHiyyíin Christian
maskíin, maskíina, masakíin poor, unfortunate; wretched
masraHíyya (masraHiyyáat) play (dramatic)
mássil, yimássil to represent; act
masṭára (masáaṭir) ruler (for school, etc.)
mas'ála (masáa'il) matter
mas'ulíyya (mas'uliyyáat) responsibility
mas'úul, mas'úula, mas'ulíin (9an) responsible (for)
maṣláHa (maṣáaliH) (Gov't) department
máṣna9 (maṣáani9) factory
maṣr Egypt; Cairo
máṣri, maṣríyya, maṣriyyíin Egyptian
mašghúul, mašghúula, mašghulíin busy, occupied
mášša, yimášši to walk s.o.
mášwi broiled
mátHaf (matáaHif) museum
matíin, matíina, mutáan strong
maṭáar (maṭaráat) airport
máṭar rain
máṭbax (maṭáabix) kitchen
máṭ9am (maṭáa9im) restaurant

mawḍúu9 (mawaḍíi9) subject, matter
mawgúud, mawgúuda, mawgudíin present
mawlúud, mawlúuda, mawludíin born
máwwit, yimáwwit to kill
máw'if (mawáa'if) stand, rank
maxṣúuṣ, maxṣúuṣa, maxṣuṣíin special
máxzan (maxáazin) place of storing
máyya water
máyyit, mayyíta, mayyitíin dead
mázza, 'mezzeh' appetizer
maẓbúuṭ, maẓbúuṭa, maẓbuṭíin correct
má9a with
ma9áad (mawa9íid) appointment
ma9áaš (ma9ašáat) pension
má9bad (ma9áabid) temple
má9dan (ma9áadin) metal
ma9lá'a (ma9áali') spoon
ma9lúum known; 'of course!'
má9mal (ma9áamil) laboratory
má9na (ma9áani) meaning
ma'áala (ma'aláat) article (e.g. in newspaper, journal)
ma'áas (ma'asáat) size
ma'áṣṣ (ma'aṣṣáat) scissors
midáan (mayadíin) city square
mifállis, mifallísa, mifallisíin bankrupt
míhna (míhan) trade, occupation
miHtáag, miHtáaga, miHtagíin (li) need(ing)
miin who?
míina (mawáani) harbour, port
mikaníiki (mikanikíyya) mechanic
miláad (mawalíid) birth
milyóon (malayíin) million
min from
minéen from where?
miráaya (marayáat) mirror
mirábba (mirabbáat) jam
mísa evening
misáafir traveller
misáa'an p.m.; in the evening

mísik, yímsik to hold, catch
miš not
míši, yímši to walk, go away
míšmiš (*c.*) apricots
mišṭ (amšáaṭ) comb
mitgáwwiz, mitgawwíza, mitgawwizíin married
míyya (miyyáat) hundred
mizáan (mawazíin) balance, scales
mizaníyya (mizaniyyáat) budget
mi'yáas in-niil Nilometer
móolid (mawáalid) saint's birthday
moot death
mooz (*c.*), **móoza** (*s.*), **(mozáat)** bananas
moxx brains
mudárris, mudarrísa, mudarrisíin teacher
múdda (múdad) period
mudíir (mudiríin) director, manager
mudiríyya (mudiriyyáat) directorate
mufáttiš, mufattíša, mufattišíin inspector
mufíid, mufíida, mufidíin useful
múfrad singular
muftáaH (mafatíiH) key
mugámma9 complex; central building of Cairo bureaucracy
mugawharáat jewelry
mugtáma9 (mugtama9áat) society
muhándis, muhandísa, (muhandisíin) engineer
muhímm, muhímma, muhimmíim important
muHáami, muHamíyya, muHamiyyíin lawyer
muHáasib, muHásba, muHasbíin accountant
muHáḍra (muHaḍaráat) lecture
muHáfẓa (muHafẓáat) governorate
muHíiṭ (muHiṭáat) ocean
muHtáram, muHtárama, muHtaramíin respected
muluxíyya (veg.) Moloukhiyya, favoured Egyptian vegetable
múmkin possible
mumtáaz, mumtáaza, mumtazíin excellent
munáasib, munásba, munasbíin appropriate
munásba (munasibáat) occasion
murúur traffic

musáa9id, musá9da, musa9díin helper, assistant
musálli, musallíyya, musalliyyíin fun, amusing
musíiqa music
múslim, muslíma, muslimíin Moslem
mustášfa (mustašfayáat) hospital
mustáwa (mustawayáat) level, standard
mustáwrad, mustawráda, mustawradíin imported
mustá'bal future
muškíla (mašáakil) problem, difficulty
múšrif, mušrífa, mušrifíin supervisor
mutárgim (mutargimíin) translator
mutašákkir, mutašakkíra, mutašakkiríin thank you
mutawássiṭ, mutawassíṭa, mutawassiṭíin medium; average
mút9ib, mut9íba, mut9ibíin tiring; tiresome
muwáHHad, muwaHHáda, muwaHHadíin unified
muwáẓẓaf, muwaẓẓáfa, muwaẓẓafíin employee
muxtálif, muxtálifa, muxtalifíin various, different
mu9állim, mu9allíma, mu9allimíin teacher
mu9á''ad, mu9a''áda, mu9a''adíin complicated; complex(ed)
mu9tádil, mu9tadíla, mu9tadilíin moderate
mú9ẓam most (of)
mu'áddab, mu'addába, mu'addabíin polite
mu'támar (mu'tamaráat) conference

n

náada, yináadi to call
náadi (nawáadi) club
naam, yináam to sleep, go to sleep
naar (niṛáan) fire
naas people
náasib, yináasib to suit
náašif, nášfa, našfíin dry
náawi, náwya, nawyíin intend(ing)
náayim, náyma, naymíin sleeping
náa'iṣ, ná'ṣa, na'ṣíin lack(ing), miss(ing)
nabáat (nabatáat) plant
nába' (anbáa') news
nábi (ánbiya) prophet

nabíih, nabíiha, núbaha intelligent
nádah, yíndah to call by shouting
náḍḍaf, yináḍḍaf to clean
náfa9, yínfa9 to be of use
nafs same
nafs (*f.*) self; soul
nagáaH success
naggáar (naggaríin) carpenter
nággaH, yinággaH to give a passing grade
naháar day(time)
nahr (anháar) river
naHl (*c.*), **náHla** (*s.*), **(naHláat)** bee
náHya (nawáaHi) side
naml (*c.*), **námla** (*s.*), **(namláat)** ant
namúus (*c.*), **namúusa** (*s.*), **(namusáat)** mosquito
nasíim breeze
náṣaH, yínṣaH to advise
naṣíib share, portion
našíiṭ, našíiṭa, nušáaṭ active, energetic
náššif, yináššif to dry (s.th.)
natíiga (natáayig) result
náṭa', yínṭa' to pronounce, utter
naṭṭ, yinúṭṭ to jump
náwwar, yináwwar to brighten, light up (s.th.)
naxl (*c.*), **náxla** (*s.*), **(naxláat)** palm-tree
náyyim, yináyyim to cause to sleep
názzil, yinázzil to bring down
naẓaríyyan theoretically
náẓẓam, yináẓẓam to organise
ná9am yes
na9náa9 mint
na9sáan, na9sáana, na9saníin sleepy
ná'al, yín'il to transfer; transport
ná'aš, yún'uš to carve, engrave
na'l transfer; transport
na'š decorating, decoration
na''áaš, na''áaša, na''ašíin painter
ná''aṣ, yiná''aṣ to decrease
ná''a, yiná''i to choose, select

nibíit wine
niḍíif, naḍíifa, niḍáaf clean
nígma (nugúum) star
niHáas copper
niháaya (nihayáat) end
niháa'i, niha'íyya, niha'iyyíin final
nimr tiger
nímra (nímar) number
nísba (nísab) proportion, percentage
nisbíyyan relatively
nísi, yínsa to forget
nízil, yínzil to descend, go down
niẓáam (núẓum) order, system
ni'áaba (ni'abáat) trade-union
noom sleep
noo9 (anwáa9) kind, sort
nufímbir November
nufúuz influence
núkta (núkat) joke
nuṣṣ half
nuṭ' pronunciation
núubi, nubíyya, nubiyyíin Nubian
nuur (anwáar) light

o

óḍa (ówaḍ) room

q

qáarin, yiqáarin to compare
qamúus (qawamíis) dictionary
qárya (qúra) village
qáwmi, qawmíyya, qawmiyyiin national
qism (aqsáam) division; department (e.g. university)
qíṣṣa (qíṣaṣ) story
qur'áan Koran

r

ráabi9 fourth
ráagil (riggáala) man
ráaHa rest, comfort
raaH, yirúuH to go, go to
ráakib, rákba, rakbíin ride (riding)
raas (ruus) head
ráayiH, ráyHa, rayHíin go(ing)
rábaṭ, yúrbuṭ to tie
rabb Lord
rábba, yirábbi to raise, bring up
rabíi9 spring (season)
radd, yirúdd (9ala) to reply to
rádyu (radyuháat) radio
ráḍa, yírḍa to please, satisfy
ráfa9, yírfa9 to lift, raise
raff (rufúuf) shelf
rágga9, yirágga9 to return (s.th.), give back
ráHHab, yiráHHab (bi) to welcome
rákkiz, yirákkiz to concentrate
ramáadi grey
ramaḍáan Ramadan
ráma, yírmi to throw
raml (rimáal) sand
rámma, yirámmi to scatter, throw away
ramz (rumúuz) symbol
rann, yirínn to ring; clink (of a coin)
rásmi, rasmíyya, rasmiyyíin official (*adj.*)
rasúul (rúsul) Messenger (of God)
raṣíif (arṣífa) pavement
ráttib, yiráttib to put in order, arrange
raṭl (arṭáal) Egyptian weight = approx. 1 lb.
ráwa, yírwi to irrigate, water
ráwwaH, yiráwwaH to go home
rayy irrigation, watering
ráyyaH, yiráyyaH to relieve
rá'aba (ri'áab) neck
rá'ad, yúr'ud to rest, take a catnap

rá'aṣ, yúr'uṣ to dance
ra'íis (rú'asa) president, chief
ra'íisi, ra'isíyya, ra'isiyyíin principal, main
rá'ṣa dance
ra'y (aráa') opinion
režíim diet
righíif (arghífa) loaf
rígi9, yírga9 to return to
rigl (rugúul) foot; leg
ríHla (riHláat) trip, journey
riif (aryáaf) country(side)
riiH (aryáaH) wind
ríiHa (rawáayiH) smell
ríiša (ríyaš) feather
ríkib, yírkab to ride, mount
rimš (rumúuš) eyelash
risáala (rasáayil) thesis
riwáaya (riwayáat) novel (*n.*)
rixíiṣ, rixíiṣa, ruxáaṣ cheap
ríxiṣ, yírxaṣ to become cheap
riyáaḍa sport(s); mathematics
rí'a lung
rub9 (arbáa9) quarter
rufáyya9, rufayyá9a, rufayya9íin thin
rugúu9 (*v.n.*) return (*intr.*)
rúkba (rúkab) knee
rukn (arkáan) corner
rukúub (*v.n.*) riding
rummáan (*c.*), **rummáana** (*s.*), **rummanáat** pomegranate
rúsya Russia
ruṭúuba humidity
ruuH (arwáaH) soul
rúumi, rumíyya, rumiyyíin European
rúusi, rusíyya, ruus Russian
rúxṣa (rúxaṣ) license
ruzz rice

s

sáabi9 seventh
sáabi', sáb'a, sab'íin preceding
saab, yisíib to leave
sáada (of coffee) without sugar
sáadis sixth
sáafir, yisáafir to travel (to)
saagh piastre
sáakin, sákna, sakníin live (living), residing
sáakin, sákna, sukkáan inhabitant
sáakit, sákta, saktíin silent
sáawa, yisáawi to equal
sáa9a (sa9áat) hour; watch, clock
sáa9id, yisáa9id to help
sáa'i9, sá'9a, sa'9íin cold (e.g. drink)
saa', yisúu' to drive
sábab (asbáab) reason, cause
sábagh, yúsbugh to dye
sábat (isbíta) basket
saba9ṭáašar seventeen
sába', yísba' to precede
sabbáak (sabbakíin) plumber
sabb, yisíbb to curse, swear
sáb9a seven
sab9íin seventy
sadd (sudúud) dam
sádda', yisádda' to believe
sáfar travel
safíir (súfara) ambassador
sággil, yisággil to record, register
sáhhil, yisáhhil to make easy, facilitate
sahl, sáhla, sahlíin easy
saHáab (*c.*), **saHáaba** (*s.*), **(súHub)** cloud
sáaHil (sawáaHil) shore
sákan, yúskun to inhabit, live
sakráan, sakráana, sakraníin drunk
saláam peace
saláama safety

sállim, yisállim to deliver; (9ála) greet; (of God) give peace or safety
sáma sky
sámaH, yísmaH (li) to allow
sámak (*c.*) fish
sammáak (sammakíin) fishmonger
sámma, yisámmi to name
sána (siníin or sanawáat) year
sanawíyya secondary (school)
sánawi, sanawíyya, sanawiyyíin annual
sandawítš (sandawitšáat) sandwich
sánya (sawáani) second (of time)
saqáafa culture
sára', yísra' to steal
saríi9, saríi9a, sari9íin fast
sáwa together
sawwáaH, sawwáaHa, sawwaHíin tourist
sawwáa' (sawwa'íin) driver
saxíif, saxíifa, súxafa silly, foolish
sáxxan, yisáxxan to heat
sáyyid (sáada) gentleman, Mr.
sa9íida hello
sa9udíyya Saudi Arabia
sa9úudi, sa9udíyya, sa9udiyyíin Saudi
sá'al, yís'al to ask
sa''áara Saqqaara
seef (suyúuf) sword
sibáaHa (*v.n.*) swimming
síbHa (síbaH) prayer-beads, rosary
sibtímbir September
sifáara (sifaaráat) embassy
sigáara (sagáayir) cigarette
siggáada (sagagíid) carpet
sign (sugúun) prison
síhir, yíshar to stay up late
síidi sir
síina Sinai
sikirtéera (sikirteráat) secretary
síkit, yúskut to be quiet

sikkíina (sakakíin) knife
síllim (saláalim) ladder
simíin, simíina, sumáan fat
sími9, yísma9 to hear
simsáar (samásra) broker
sínima (sinimáat) cinema
sinn age
sinna (sináan) tooth
sír'a theft
siríir (saráayir) bed
sitáara (satáayir) curtain
sitt (sittáat) woman
sítta six
siṭṭáašar sixteen
sittíin sixty
siyáasa (siyasáat) politics; policy
siyáasi, siyasíyya, siyasiyyíin political
si9r (as9áar) price
sudáan Sudan
súfra dining table
sufragi (sufragíyya) butler
suhúula ease
suHúur daily pre-fast meal in Ramadan
súkkar (*c.*) sugar
surúur pleasure
súrya Syria
súr9a speed
súuri, suríyya, suriyyíin Syrian
suu' evil
suu' (aswáa') market
suxn, súxna, suxníin hot
suxxáan (suxxanáat) water heater
su'áal (as'íla) question

ṣ

ṣáafi, ṣáfya, ṣafyíin clear (e.g. weather)
ṣáaHib (aṣHáab) friend; owner
ṣáala (ṣaláat) hall

ṣáaliH, yisáaliH to make up with
ṣaam, yiṣúum to fast
ṣabáaH morning
ṣabáaHan in the morning, a.m.
ṣábar, yúṣbur to be patient
ṣabb, yiṣúbb to pour
ṣábi, ṣabíyya (ṣubyáan) young boy or girl
ṣabr patience
ṣabúun soap
ṣádaf (*c.*) sea-shells
ṣadr chest (anatomy)
ṣaff (ṣufúuf) row
ṣáffar, yiṣáffar to whistle
ṣáfHa (ṣafaHáat) page
ṣafíiHa (ṣafáayiH) large tin
ṣáHba (ṣaHbáat) (*f.*) friend; (*f.*) owner
ṣaHH, yiṣáHH to be correct (*3rd pers. s. only*)
ṣaHiiH correct
ṣaHn (ṣuHúun) plate, dish
ṣáHra desert
ṣaHráawi, ṣaHrawíyya, ṣaHrawiyyíin desert (*adj.*)
ṣaHw, ṣáHwa clear (weather)
ṣala prayer
ṣálaṭa salad
ṣállaH, yiṣállaH to repair
ṣálla, yiṣálli to pray
ṣána9, yíṣna9 to manufacture
ṣándal (ṣanadíil) sandal(s)
ṣaníyya (ṣawáani) tray
ṣánṭi centimeter
ṣaráaHa frankness
ṣáraf, yíṣrif to spend
ṣarráaf (ṣarrafíin) money changer; cashier
ṣarúux (ṣawaríix) rocket
ṣaṭH (suṭúuH) roof
ṣaṭr (ṣuṭúur) line (e.g. of text)
ṣáwwar, yiṣáwwar to photograph
ṣaxr (ṣuxúur) rock
ṣaydáli (ṣaydalíyya) pharmacist

ṣáyyif, yiṣáyyif to spend the summer
ṣa9b, ṣá9ba, ṣa9bíin difficult
ṣa9íidi, ṣa9idíyya, ṣa9áyda Upper Egyptian
ṣá99ab, yiṣá99ab to make (s.th.) difficult
ṣeef summer
ṣíHHa health
ṣiin China
ṣináa9a (ṣina9aat) industry
ṣináa9i, ṣina9íyya, ṣina9iyyíin industrial
ṣiyáam (*v.n.*) fasting
ṣoom fasting
ṣoot (aṣwáat) voice; vote
ṣubáa9 (ṣawáabi9) finger; toe
ṣubH morning
ṣudáa9 head-ache
ṣúdfa chance
ṣugháyyar, ṣughayyára, ṣughayyaríin small; young
ṣúHafi (ṣuHafiyyíin) journalist
ṣulH peace
ṣulṭáan (ṣalaṭíin) Sultan
ṣuuf wool
ṣúufi Sufi
ṣúura (ṣúwar) picture, photograph
ṣu9úuba difficulty

š

šaab (šabáab) young man
šaaf, yišúuf to see
šaal, yišíil to carry; remove
šáari9 (šawáari9) street
šáaṭir, šáṭra, šuṭṭáar clever
šáaṭi' (šawáaṭi') beach
šaay tea
šáayif, šáyfa, šayfíin seeing
šábaka (šabakáat) net
šadd, yišídd to pull
šáfa, yíšfi to recover, be cured
šagáa9a courage

šágar (*c.*), **šágara** (*s.*), **(ašgáar)** tree(s)
šágga9, yišágga9 to encourage
šaghgháal, šaghgháala, šaghghalíin working
šághghal, yišághghal to operate
šaháada (šahadáat) certificate
šáHat, yíšHat to beg
šáHHat, yišáHHat to give to a beggar
šaHm grease
šaHn (*v.n.*) loading
šahr (áššhur *or* **šuhúur)** month
šáhri, šahríyya, šahriyyíin monthly
šákar, yúškur to thank
šakk (šukúuk) doubt
šakl (aškáal) shape
šákwa (šakáawi) complaint
šamáal north
šamm, yišímm to smell (s.th.)
šams (*f.*) sun
šam9 wax
šám9a (šam9áat) candle
šánṭa (šúnaṭ) suitcase, bag, briefcase
šaráab (šarabáat) socks
šáraf honour
šáraH, yíšraH to explain
šaríik (šúraka) partner
šarr evil
šárraf, yišárraf to honour
šarṭ (šurúuṭ) condition
šar' east
šár'i, šar'íyya, šar'iyyíin eastern(er)
šataráng chess
šáwa, yíšwi to grill
šawíiš (šawišíyya) sergeant
šaxṣ (ašxáaṣ) person
šaxṣíyya (šaxṣiyyáat) personality
šáxṣi, šaxṣíyya, šaxṣiyyíin personal, private
šayyáal (šayyalíin) porter
ša9b (šu9úub) people, folk
ša9bi, ša9bíyya, ša9biyyíin popular, of the common people

ša9r hair
šá''a (šú'a') apartment
šeex (šuyúux) sheikh
šee' (ašyáa') thing
šibbáak (šababíik) window
šíbšib (šabáašib) slippers
šiik (šikáat) cheque
šimáal left (-hand side)
šírib, yíšrab to drink
širíiṭ (šaráayiṭ) tape; cassette
šírka (šarikáat) company
šíta winter
ši9r poetry
šóoka (šúwak) fork
šugáa9, šugáa9a, šug9áan brave
šughl work
šukr thanks, gratitude
šúkran thank you
šurb (*v.n.*) drinking
šúrba soup
šwáyya a little; slowly

t

taag (tigáan) crown
táagir (tuggáar) merchant, trader
táalit, tálta third
táamin, támna eighth
táani again
táani, tánya second
táani, tánya, tanyíin other
táasi9, tás9a ninth
tába9, yítba9 to follow
tadríib training
tadxíin smoking
tafáahum (mutual) understanding
tafkíir thinking
tafṣíil (tafaṣíil) detail
tagdíid renewal

taghyíir change (*trans.*)
taHíyya (taHiyyáat) greeting(s)
taHríir liberation
taHsíin improvement
taHt under
takábbur haughtiness
takmíla completion
takríir repeating; refining
taks taxi
taláata three
talatíin thirty
talaṭṭáašar thirteen
talg ice; snow
talláaga (tallagáat) refrigerator
tamáam exactly
táman (atmáan) price
tamanṭáašar eighteen
tamánya eight
tamríin (tamrináat) drill, exercise
tanḍíif cleaning
tanẓíim organising
taqlíid (taqalíid) tradition, convention
tárgim, yitárgim to translate
targumáan interpreter, 'dragoman'
taríix (tawaríix) date; history
tartíib arrangement
tár'iya promotion
tasgíil recording (e.g. words, music), registering
tashíil (tashiláat) facility; facilitating, making easy
tawzíi9 distribution
taxáṣṣuṣ specialization
taxzíin storing
tazkára (tazáakir) ticket
ta9áala (-i, -u) come!
ta9báan, ta9báana, ta9baníin tired; sick
tá9lab (ta9áalib) fox
ta9líim (ta9limáat) instruction(s); teaching
ta9líiq commentary
ta9ríifa half-piastre

ta'ríiban approximately
ta'ríir (ta'aríir) report
tigáara trade, commerce
tiin (*c.*) figs
tilifóon (tilifonáat) telephone
tilivizyóon (tilivizyonáat) television
tilmíiz (talámza) pupil, student
tilmíiza (tilmizáat) (*f.*) pupil, student
tilt (atláat) third
timsáal (tamasíil) statue
tír9a (tíra9) channel, irrigation canal
tisa9ṭáašar nineteen
tís9a nine
tis9íin ninety
tixíin, tixíina, tuxáan fat
tí9ib, yít9ab to get tired
ti'íil, ti'íila, tu'áal heavy
toom (*c.*) garlic
tuffáaH (*c.*), **tuffáaHa** (*s.*), **(tuffaHáat)** apple
tugáari, tugaríyya, tugariyyíin commercial
turáab dust
turkíiya Turkey
túrki, turkíyya, (atráak) Turk(ish)
turmáay (turmayáat) tram(way), streetcar

ṭ

ṭáabi9 (ṭawáabi9) stamp
ṭáalib (ṭulláab or ṭálaba) student
ṭáaliba (ṭalibáat) (*f.*) student
ṭaar, yiṭíir to fly
ṭáaza (invar.) fresh (of food)
ṭábax, yúṭbux to cook
ṭába' (aṭbáa') plate
ṭabbáax, ṭabbáaxa, ṭabbaxíin cook
ṭabíib (aṭibbáa') doctor
ṭabíi9a nature
ṭabíi9i, ṭabi9íyya, ṭabi9iyyíin natural
ṭabúur (ṭawabíir) queue, line (of people)

ṭabx (*v.n.*) cooking
ṭáb9an of course
ṭáfa, yíṭfi to extinguish, put out; turn off
ṭaffáaya (ṭaffayáat) ashtray
ṭálab (ṭalabáat) request, demand; application
ṭálab, yúṭlub to demand, ask for, order (in a restaurant)
ṭálla', yiṭálla' divorce
ṭáma9 greed
ṭammáa9, ṭammáa9a, ṭamma9íin greedy
ṭaqs weather
ṭaráawa softness; coolness (weather)
ṭarabéeza (ṭarabezáat) table
ṭarbúuš (ṭarabiiš) tarboosh, fez
ṭard (ṭurúud) parcel
ṭaríi' (ṭúru') way
ṭaríi'a (ṭúru') means, method
ṭawíil, ṭawíila, ṭuwáal tall, long
ṭáwla backgammon
ṭawwáali straight ahead
ṭayaráan (*v.n.*) aviation, flying
ṭayyáara (ṭayyaráat) airplane
ṭáyyib all right, okay
ṭáyyib, ṭayyíba, ṭayyibíin good
ṭa9míyya felafel, a deep-fried vegetable dish
ṭá99am, yiṭá99am to inlay
ṭibb (the field of) medicine
ṭifl (aṭfáal) child
ṭiHíina tahina, sesame paste
ṭiin mud
ṭíli9, yíṭla9 to climb, go up
ṭuul length

u

'uddáam in front of
úghniya (agháani) song
úgra fee, fare
ukazyóon (ukazyonáat) sale (at reduced prices)
uktóobar October

'uláyyil, 'ulayyíla, 'ulayyilíin little (amount)
'umáaš cloth
umm (ummaháat) mother
unbúuba (anabíib) pipe (plumbing)
urúbba Europe
urúbbi, urubbíyya, urubbiyyíin European
usbúu9 (asabíi9) week
uslúub (asalíib)
úsṭa (used to address taxi drivers, etc.)
ustáaz (asátza) professor
utubíis (utubisáat) bus
úula (*f.*) first
'urάyyib near, soon
'uṣáyyar, 'uṣayyára, 'uṣayyaríin short
'úuṭa (*c.*) tomatoes
uxt (ixwáat) sister

w

wáadi (widyáan) valley
wáaḍiH, wáḍHa, waḍHíin clear
wáafi', yiwáafi' (9ála) to agree (on)
wáagib (wagibáat) duty; homework
wáaHid (wáHda) one
wáalid father
wáasi9, wás9a, was9íin wide, spacious
wáaṭi, wáṭya, waṭyíin low
wáaxid, wáxda, waxdíin (have) taken
wáa'if, wá'fa, wa'fíin stop(ping); stand(ing)
wádda9, yiwádda9 to bid farewell, see off
wádda, yiwáddi to take to a place, deliver
wáḍḍab, yiwáḍḍab to arrange; pack (a suitcase)
wáffar, yiwáffar to save (e.g. money)
wága9, yíwga9 to hurt
wáHaš, yíwHaš to be missed by
wálad (awláad) boy; son
wálda mother
wálla or
walláa9a (walla9áat) (cigarette-)lighter

wálla9, yiwálla9 to light, ignite; switch on
wára behind
wára' (*c.*) **wára'a** (*s.*), **(awráa')** paper
ward (*c.*), **wárda** (*s.*), **wardáat** flower
wárra, yiwárri to show
wárša (wíraš) workshop
wasíila (wasáa'il) method
wasṭáani, wasṭaníyya, wasṭaniyyíin intermediate
wásṭa someone who can pull strings for you
wáṣṣal, yiwáṣṣal to take somewhere, deliver
wáṭan (awṭáan) native country
wáṭṭa, yiwáṭṭi to lower (e.g. volume)
wáxri, waxríyya, waxriyyíin late
wáyya with
wázan, yíwzin to weigh (trans.)
wazíir (wúzara) minister
wázza9, yiwázza9 to distribute
wá9ad, yíw9id to promise
wá'a9, yú'a9 to fall
wa't time
wá''af, yiwá''af to stop
wi and
widn (*f.*), **(widáan)** ear
wíHiš, wíHša, wiHšíin bad; ugly
wíldit, tíwlid to give birth
wíli9, yíwla9 to catch fire, be lit
wísix, wísxa, wisxíin dirty
wíṣil, yíwṣal to arrive (at)
wišš (wušúuš) face
wizáara (wizaráat) ministry
wizz (*c.*) goose
wí'if, yú'af to stop; stand up
wi-Hyáat(ak, etc.) please
wuḍúuH clarity
wugúud presence, existence
wuṣúul arrival

x

xaaf, yixáaf (**min**) to be afraid of; (**9ála**) be afraid for
xaal (xiláan) maternal uncle
xáala (xaláat) aunt
xáaliṣ extremely
xaam raw, crude
xáamis fifth
xáani', yixáani' to quarrel
xáarig outside
xaaṣṣ, xáaṣṣa, xaṣṣíin special; private
xáatim (xawáatim) ring (for finger)
xáayif, xáyfa, xayfíin afraid
xábar (axbáar) news
xabbáaz, xabbáaza, xabbazíin baker
xábbar, yixábbar to inform
xábbaṭ, yixábbaṭ (9aléehum) to knock (at s.o.'s door)
xabíir (xúbara) expert
xádam, yíxdim to serve
xaddáam, xaddáama, xaddamíin servant
xad, yáaxud to take
xaff, yixíff to become light (weight); to get well
xafíif, xafíifa, xufáaf light(weight)
xaláaṣ finished; agreed, okay
xála', yíxla' to create
xalíifa (*m.*), **(xúlafa)** caliph
xalíig (xulgáan) gulf
xall vinegar
xállaṣ, yixállaṣ to finish
xálla, yixálli to let, leave, allow
xamasíin the Khamseen (wind and sandstorm)
xamasṭáašar fifteen
xámra (xumúur) wine
xámsa five
xamsíin fifty
xanzíir (xanaziir) pig, pork
xárag, yúxrug to go out
xarbáan, xarbáana, xarbaníin broken (down); out of order
xárbiš, yixárbiš to scratch

xaríif autumn
xaríiṭa (xaráayiṭ) map
xarúuf (xirfáan) sheep
xaṣṣ (*c.*) lettuce
xass, yixíss to lose weight
xášab (*c.*) wood
xášabi, xašabíyya, xašabiyyíin wooden
xašš, yixúšš to enter
xátam, yíxtim to stamp, frank
xáṭab, yúxṭub to get engaged to
xaṭar (axṭáar) danger
xaṭṭ (xuṭúuṭ) hand-writing, calligraphy
xaṭṭáaṭ (xaṭṭaṭíin) calligrapher
xawáaga (xawagáat) foreign gentleman
xáwwif, yixáwwif to frighten
xayyáaṭa (xayyaṭáat) seamstress
xáyyaṭ, yixáyyaṭ to sew
xáyyim, yixáyyim to pitch a tent
xeel (*c.*) horses
xeer good(ness)
xíbra experience
xídma (xadamáat) service
xígil, yíxgal to be ashamed, embarrassed
xíliṣ, yíxlaṣ to end, be finished
xiyáar (*c.*) cucumber
xoox (*c.*) peaches
xuḍáar vegetables
xums one-fifth
xumsumíyya five hundred
xusáara (xasaayir) loss
xuṣúuṣan especially
xuṣúuṣi, xuṣuṣíyya, xuṣuṣiyyíin

y

ya O . . . (*vocative*)
yabáan Japan
yabáani, yabaníyya, yabaniyyíin Japanese
yádawi, yadawíyya, yadawiyyíin handmade

yadd [= iid] (*f.*) hand
yahúudi, yahudíyya, yahúud Jew(ish)
yálla let's go; hurry up!
yanáayir January
yaréet would that it were so
yatára I wonder if . . .
yá9ni it means; in other words
yimíin right (-hand side)
yoom (ayyáam) day
yúlyu July
yunáan Greece
yunnáani, yunaníyya, yunaniyyíin Greek
yúnyu June

z

zaad, yizíid to increase (*intr.*)
záakir, yizáakir to study
zaar, yizúur to visit
záayir, záyra, zuwwáar visitor
záHma crowd; crowded (invar.)
zamáan time; long ago
zára9, yízra9 to plant, cultivate
zatúun olives
záwwid, yizáwwid to (cause to) increase
zayy like
zayy ma just like
zá9al anger
za9láan, za9láana, za9laníin angry
zá99al, yizá99al to anger
zá99a', yizá99a' (li) to shout at
za'', yizú'' to push
zeet (zuyúut) oil
zibáala garbage
zíbda butter
zibúun, zibúuna, zabáayin customer
zift tar; (*idiom.*) terrible
zíhi', yízha' (min) to get bored of
zíina (zináat) decoration

zimíil (zúmala) colleague
ziráa9a agriculture
ziráa9i, zira9íyya, zira9iyyíin agricultural
ziyáada (ziyadáat) increase
ziyáara (ziyaráat) visit
zí9il, yíz9al **(min)** to be angry with; **(9ála)** feel sorry for
zukáam (head-)cold
zu'áa' alley

ẓ

ẓáabiṭ (ẓubbaaṭ) officer
ẓábaṭ, yúẓbuṭ to control; set (a watch)
ẓáhar, yíẓhar to appear
ẓálam, yíẓlim or **yúẓlum** to oppress
ẓann, yiẓúnn or **yiẓínn** to think (that); be of the opinion
ẓarf (ẓurúuf) envelope
ẓulm tyranny

9

9a (= 9ála) on
9áada (9adáat) habit, custom
9áadatan usually
9áadi, 9adíyya, 9adiyyíin ordinary, usual
9aad, yi9íid to repeat, do again
9aag ivory
9áakis, yi9áakis to tease, bother; flirt with
9áalam world
9áali, 9álya, 9alyíin high
9aam, yi9úum to swim
9aam (a9wáam) year
9áamil (9ummáal) worker
9áamil, yi9áamil to treat
9áamil, 9ámla, 9amlíin do(ing), make (making)
9aamm, 9áamma public, general
9áarif, 9árfa, 9arfíin know(ing)
9aaṣífa (9awáaṣif) storm
9aaš, yi9iiš to live

9áawiz, 9áwza, 9awzíin want(ing)
9áayiz, 9áyza, 9ayzíin want(ing)
9aaz, yi9úuz to want, need
9abíiṭ, 9abíiṭa, 9ubṭ stupid, idiotic
9add (a9dáad) number
9addáad (9addadáat) meter (e.g., of a taxi)
9ádda, yi9áddi to cross; exceed
9add, yi9ídd to count
9ads lentils
9adúuw (a9daa') enemy
9aḍḍ, yi9úḍḍ to bite (of animals & insects)
9aḍm (*c.*) bone
9áfa, yí9fi (min) to exempt from
9afríiṭ (9afaríiṭ) demon, imp; naughty child
9afš luggage
9áfwan Don't mention it (resp. to **šukran**)
9ágab, yí9gib to please
9ágala (9agaláat) bicycle
9agúuz (9awagíiz) old man
9aẓíim, 9aẓíima, 9uẓáam great
9aks opposite
9ála on
9álam (a9láam) flag
9alašáan because, for, in order to
9állim, yi9állim to teach
9ámal work
9amalíyya (9amaliyyáat) operation
9amalíyyan practically
9ámali, 9amalíyya, 9amaliyyíin practical
9ámal, yí9mil to do, make
9amm (9imáam) paternal uncle
9ámma (9ammáat) paternal aunt
9an about
9and at, 'chez'
9arabíyya (9arabiyyáat) car, automobile
9árabi, 9arabíyya, 9árab Arab, Arabic
9ára' sweat
9arbági (9arbagíyya) driver (of horse and carriage)
9arḍ (9urúuḍ) offer

9aríis (9irsáan) bridegroom
9árraf, yi9árraf to introduce
9arúusa (9aráayis) bride; doll
9ásal honey
9áskari (9asáakir) policeman; soldier
9áṣab (a9ṣáab) nerve
9aṣábi, 9aṣabíyya, 9aṣabiyyíin nervous
9áṣar, yí9ṣur to squeeze
9aṣíir juice
9aṣr (9uṣúur) era
9áša dinner
9ašáan because, for, in order to
9ášara ten
9átša, yi9átši to give dinner
9áṭaš thirst
9aṭláan, 9aṭláana, 9aṭlaníin out of order
9aṭšáan, 9aṭšáana, 9aṭšaníin thirsty
9áṭṭal, yi9áṭṭal to obstruct
9áwwim, yi9áwwim to cause to swim
9ayyáan, 9ayyáana, 9ayyaníin sick, ill
9áyyaṭ, yi9áyyaṭ to cry, weep
9áyyin, yi9áyyin to appoint
9ázam, yí9zim (9ála) to invite (for)
9ázzil, yi9ázzil to move in (to a new residence)
9a'd (9u'úud) contract
9á'rab (9a'áarib) scorpion
9eeb shame
9éela (9eláat) family
9een (9uyúun) eye
9eeš bread
9ibáara (9ibaráat) expression
9iid (a9yáad) festival, holiday
9iláa'a (9ila'áat) relation
9ílba (9ílab) small tin or box
9ílmi, 9ilmíyya, 9ilmiyyíin scientific
9imáara (9imaráat) building
9ínab (*c.*) grapes
9inwáan (9anawíin) address, title
9iráa': il-9iráa' Iraq

9iráa'i, 9ira'íyya, 9ira'iyyíin Iraqi
9írif, yí9raf to know
9išríin twenty
9iṭiš, yí9ṭaš to get thirsty
9iyáada (9iyadáat) doctor's office
9íyi, yí9ya to get ill
9izz honour, glory
9oom (*v.n.*) swimming
9uḍw (a9dáa') member
9úmda (9úmad) headman (in village)
9umr life(time)
9umúuman generally
9uzúuma (9uzumáat) invitation; dinner party
9u'báal(-ak), etc.) May (you) be next

ENGLISH–ARABIC GLOSSARY

a

able ’áadir; to be able ’ídir, yí’dar
about 9an (= concerning); Hawáali (= approximately)
above foo’
absent gháayib; **to be absent** ghaab, yighíib
to accept ’íbil, yí’bal
accident Hádsa (Hawáadis)
account Hisáab (Hisabáat)
accountant muHáasib, muHásba, muHasbíin
accustomed to mit9áwwid, mit9awwída, mit9awwidíin 9ála
to act (on stage) mássil, yimássil
acting tamsiil
active našiiṭ, našíiṭa, nušáaṭ
actor mumássil (mumássiliin)
address 9inwáan (9anawíin)
administration idáara
to advise náṣaH, yínṣaH
afraid xáayif, xáyfa, xayfíin; **to be afraid** xaaf, yixáaf
after ba9d; ba9d ma + *v.*
afternoon ba9d iḍ-ḍuhr
afterwards ba9déen
again táani; márra tánya
against ḍidd
age sinn; 9umr
to agree ittáfa’, yittífi’
agricultural ziráa9i, zira9íyya, zira9iyyíin
agriculture ziráa9a
air háwa
airmail baríid gáwwi
airplane ṭayyáara (ṭayyaráat)
airport maṭáar (maṭaráat)
air-conditioner mukáyyif háwa
Alexandria iskindiríyya
all kull; gamíi9
also bárḍu; kamáan
although ma9’ínn
always dáyman

ambassador safíir (súfara)
amber kahramáan
America amríika
American amrikáani, amrikaníyya, amrikáan
amount máblagh (mabáaligh)
ancient 'adíim, 'adíima, 'udáam
and wi or wa
angry za9láan, za9láana, za9laníin; (**to be angry** =) zí9il, yíz9al
animal Hayawáan (Hayawanáat)
annual sánawi, sanawíyya, sanawiyyíin
another táani
answer gawáab (agwíba); **to answer** gáawib, yigáawib
antique antíika (antikáat)
antiquities asáar
any ayy
anyway 9ála kull Haal
apartment šá''a (šú'a')
apples tuffáaH (*c.*)
application (form) istimáara (istimaráat)
appointment ma9áad (mawa9íid)
to approach 'árrab, yi'árrab
apricots mišmiš (*c.*)
April abríil
Arab 9árabi, 9arabíyya, 9árab
area manṭí'a (manáaṭi')
arm diráa9 (adrí9a)
armpit baaṭ (baṭáat)
army geeš (guyúuš)
to arrange ráttib, yiráttib
to arrest 'ábaḍ, yí'baḍ (9ála)
arrival wuṣúul
to arrive wíṣil, yíwṣal
art fann (funúun)
ashtray ṭaffáaya (ṭaffayáat)
to ask (a question =) sá'al, yís'al; (**to ask for** =) ṭálab, yúṭlub
asleep náayim, náyma, naymíin
assembly máglis (magáalis)
assistance musá9da
assistant musáa9id, musá9da, musa9díin

astonished mistághrab, mistaghrába, mistaghrabíin
at 9and
atmosphere gaww
to attempt Háawil, yiHáawil; (n. =) muHáwla
to attend Híḍir, yíHḍar
attractive gazzáab, gazzáaba, gazzabíin
August ughúsṭus
aunt (maternal =) xáala (xaláat); **(paternal =)** 9ámma (9ammáat)
autumn xaríif
awake ṣáaHi, sáHya, saHyíin

b

back ḍahr (ḍuhúur)
backgammon ṭáwla
bad wíHiš, wíHša, wiHšíin
bag (handbag, briefcase, suitcase =) šánṭa (šúnaṭ); **(paperbag =)** kiis (akyáas)
baksheesh ba'šíiš
balcony balakóona (balakonáat)
bananas mooz (*c.*)
bank bank (bunúuk)
bankrupt mifállis, mifallísa, mifallisíin; **to be bankrupt** fállis, yifállis
bar baar (baráat)
barber Halláa' (Halla'íin)
barefoot Háafi, Háfya, Hafyíin
to bargain fáaṣil, yifáaṣil
bargaining fiṣáal
barrel barmíil (baramíil)
to base ássis, yi'ássis
basic asáasi, asasíyya, asasiyyíin
basis asáas (úsus)
basket sábat (isbíta)
bathroom Hammáam (Hammamáat); **(toilet =)** it-twalétt
to be kaan, yikúun
beans fuul; faṣúlya
beard da'n (*f.*) (du'úun)

to beat (hit =) ḍárab, yíḍrib; **(defeat =)** ghálab, yíghlib

beautiful gamíil, gamíila, gumáal

because li'ínn; 9ašáan; 9alašáan; aṣl

to become bá'a, yíb'a

bed siríir (saráayir)

bedroom oḍt in-noom (úwaḍ in-noom)

beer bíira

bees naHl (*c.*)

before 'abl; 'abl ma (+ *v.*)

to beg šáHat, yíšHat

beggar šaHHáat (šaHHatíin)

to begin ibtáda, yibtídi

beginning bidáaya

behind wára

to believe sádda', yisádda'

bell gáras (agráas)

belonging to bitáa9, bitá9t, bitúu9

below taHt

belt Hizáam (aHzíma)

benefit fáyda (fawáayid)

to benefit (*tr.*) faad, yifíid; (intr.) istafáad, yistafíid min

beside (next to =) gamb

between been

bicycle 9ágala (9agaláat)

big kibíir, kibíira, kubáar

bill Hisáab (Hisabáat)

birth miláad (mawalíid)

to bite (animal =) 9aḍḍ, yi9úḍḍ; **(insect =)** 'áraṣ, yú'ruṣ

black íswid, sóoda, suud

'black market' is-suu' is-sóoda

to bless báarik, yibáarik

blessing báraka

blind á9ma, 9ámya, 9umy

blood damm

blow ḍárba (ḍarbáat)

blue ázra', zár'a, zur'

boat márkib (maráakib)

body gism (agsáam)

to boil ghála, yíghli

bones 9aḍm (*c.*)
book kitáab (kútub)
booking Hagz
bookstore maktába (makáatib)
boring mumíll, mumílla, mumillíin
born mawlúud; **(to be born =)** itwálad, yitwílid
to borrow istálaf, yistílif
bottle 'izáaza ('azáayiz)
boundary Hadd (Hudúud)
box 9ílba (9ílab); ṣandúu' (ṣanadíi')
boy wálad (awláad or wiláad)
bracelet iswíra (asáawir)
brain dimáagh; muxx (imxáax)
branch far9 (furúu9)
bread 9eeš
to break (*tr.*) kásar, yíksar; (*intr.*) inkásar, yinkísir
breakfast fuṭúur; **to eat breakfast** fíṭir, yífṭar
bridge kúbri (kabáari)
briefcase šánṭa (šúnaṭ)
to bring gaab, yigíib; **(bring!)** haat, háati, háatu
broadcasting izáa9a
broken maksúur
broken(down) xarbáan, xarbáana, xarbaníin; 9aṭláan, 9aṭláana, 9atlaníin
brother axx (ixwáat)
brown búnni; ásmar, sámra, sumr
brush fúrša (fúraš)
budget mizaníyya (mizaniyyáat)
bugs ba''
building bináaya (binayáat); 9imáara (9imaráat)
to burn Hára', yíHra'
bus utubíis (utubisáat)
busy mašghúul, mašghúula, mašghulíin
but láakin
butagaz butagáaz
butcher gazzáar (gazzaríin)
butter zíbda
to buy ištára, yištíri
buying šíra
by bi

c

cabbage(s) kurúmb (*c.*)
café 'áhwa ('aháawi)
Cairo maṣr; il-qaahíra
to calculate Hásab, yíHsib
to call náada, yináadi; **(to telephone =)** ḍárab, yíḍrab tilifóon li; **(to name =)** sámma, yisámmi
calm háadi, hádya, hadyíin
camel gámal, gimáal
camera kámira (kamiráat)
canal tír9a (tíra9)
candle šám9a (šam9áat)
car 9arabíyya (9arabiyyáat)
card biṭáa'a (biṭa'áat)
carpenter naggáar (naggaríin)
carpet siggáada (sagagíid)
carriage (buggy =) Hanṭúur (Hanaṭíir)
carrots gázar (*c.*)
to carry šaal, yišíil
cashier ṣarráaf (ṣarrafíin)
cat 'úṭṭa ('úṭaṭ)
to catch mísik, yímsik
cause sábab (asbáab)
ceiling sa'f
celebration iHtifáal
certain (sure =) muta'ákkid, muta'akkída, muta'akkidíin; **(specific =)** mu9áyyan
chair kursi (karáasi)
change g͟háyyar, yig͟háyyar; (*v.n.*) tag͟hyíir; **(money =)** fákka
chapter faṣl (fuṣúul)
cheap rixíiṣ, rixíiṣa, ruxáaṣ
cheese gíbna
cheque šiik (šikáat)
chess šataráng
chicken firáax (*c.*)
children wiláad or awláad; 9iyáal
chin da'n (*f.*) (du'úun)
China iṣ-ṣiin
choice ixtiyáar

to choose ixtáar, yixtáar
Christian masíiHi, masiHíyya, masiHiyyíin
church kiníisa (kanáayis)
cigarette sigáara (sagáayir)
cinema sínima (sinimáat)
Citadel il-'ál9a
city madíina (múdun)
city square midáan (mayadíin)
civilization Haḍáara (Haḍaráat)
Classical Arabic il-fúṣHa
clean niḍíif
to clean náḍḍaf, yináḍḍaf
cleaning tanḍíif
clever šáaṭir, šáṭra, šatríin
clock sáa9a (sa9áat)
to close 'áfal, yí'fil
cloth 'umáaš
clothes hudúum; maláabis
clouds saHáab (*c.*)
club (social =) náadi (nawáadi)
coast sáaHil (sawáaHil)
coat bálṭu (baláaṭi)
coffee 'áhwa
cold bard
colleague zimíil (zúmala)
college kullíyya (kulliyyáat)
Colloquial Arabic il-lúgha d-dáariga; il-lúgha l-9ammíyya
colour loon (alwáan)
comb mišṭ (amšáaṭ)
to come ga, yíigi
coming gaay, gáaya, gayíin
commotion dáwša
company šírka (šarikáat)
to complain ištáka, yištíki
to complete kámmil, yikámmil
complex mi9á''ad, mi9a''áda, mi9a''adíin
to concentrate rákkiz, yirákkiz 9ála
condition Haal (aHwáal); **(requirement =)** šarṭ (šurúuṭ)
congratulations mabrúuk

continue istamárr, yistamírr; 'á9ad, yú'9ud + imperf.
cook ṭabbáax (ṭabbaxíin)
cooking ṭabx
Copt(ic) 'íbṭi, 'ibṭíyya, a'báaṭ
correct ṣaHíiH
cotton 'uṭn
council máglis (magáalis)
to count 9add, yi9ídd
country bálad (*f.*) (biláad)
crazy magnúun (maganíin)
cream 'íšṭa
crescent hiláal
to cross 9ádda, yi9áddi
crow ghuráab (ghirbáan)
crowd záHma
crown taag (tigáan)
cucumber xiyáar (*c.*)
culture saqáafa
cup fingáan (fanagíin)
cupboard duláab (dawalíib)
curtain sitáara (satáayir)
Customs gúmruk (gamáarik)
to cut 'áṭa9, yí'ṭa9; **(into many pieces =)** 'áṭṭa9, yi'áṭṭa9

d

dam sadd (sudúud)
to dance rá'aṣ, yúr'uṣ
dancer (*f.*) ra''áaṣa (ra''aṣáat)
danger xáṭar (axṭáar)
darkness ḍaláam
date taríix (tawaríix)
dawn fagr
day yoom (ayyáam)
daytime naháar
dead máyyit, mayyíta, mayyitíin
deaf áṭraš, ṭárša, ṭurš
December disímbir
degree dáraga (daragáat)

to delay 'áxxar, yi'áxxar
to deliver sállim, yisállim; wáṣṣal, yiwáṣṣal
to demand ṭálab, yúṭlub
department qism (aqsáam)
to descend nízil, yínzil
desk máktab (makáatib)
dialect láhga (lahgáat)
diarrhoea isháal
dictionary qamúus (qawamíis)
to die maat, yimúut
to differ ixtálaf, yixtílif
different muxtálif, muxtálifa, muxtalifíin
difficult ṣa9b, ṣá9ba, ṣa9bíin
difficulty ṣu9úuba
dinner 9áša
diplomat(ic) diblumáasi, diblumasíyya, diblumasiyyíin
director mudíir (mudiríin)
dirty wísix, wísxa, wisxíin
disease máraḍ (amráaḍ)
dish ṭába' (aṭbáa')
distance bu9d
to disturb dáayi', yidáayi'
to divorce ṭalla', yiṭálla'
to do 9ámal, yí9mil
doctor duktóor (dakátra); ṭabíib (aṭibbáa')
dog kalb (kiláab)
doing 9áamil, 9ámla, 9amlíin
donkey Humáar (Himíir)
door baab (abwáab)
doorman bawwáab (bawwabíin)
down taht
drawer durg (adráag)
dress fustáan (fasatíin)
to drink šírib, yíšrab
drinking šurb
to drive saa', yisúu'
driver sawwáa' (sawwa'íin)
drunk sakráan, sakráana, sakraníin
dumb áxras, xársa, xurs
duty wáagib (wagibáat)

e

ear widn (*f.*) (widáan)
early bádri
earth arḍ (*f.*)
ease suhúula
east šar'
eastern(er) šár'i, šar'íyya, šar'iyyíin
easy sahl, sáhla, sahlíin
to eat ákal or kal, yáakul
eggplant bitingáan (*c.*)
eggs beeḍ (*c.*)
Egypt maṣr
Egyptian máṣri, maṣríyya, maṣriyyíin
electricity kahrába
election intixáab, intixabáat
elephant fiil
embarrassed maksúuf, maksúufa, maksufíin
embassy sifáara (sifaráat)
employee muwáẓẓaf (muwaẓẓafíin)
empty fáaḍi, fáḍya, faḍyíin
to end intáha, yintíhi; (*n.*) intiháa'
engineer muhándis (muhandisíin)
England ingiltíra
English ingilíizi, ingilizíyya, ingilíiz
enough kifáaya
to enter dáxal, yúdxul; xašš, yixúšš
entering (*v.n.*) duxúul
envelope ẓarf, ẓurúuf
Europe urúbba
European urúbbi, urubbíyya, urubbiyyíin
evening mísa
every kull
exactly biẓ-ẓábṭ
examination imtiHáan (imtiHanáat)
example másal (amsíla)
except ílla
to excuse sámaH, yísmaH
existence wugúud
to expect intáẓar, yintíẓir

expecting intiẓáar
expensive gháali, ghálya, ghalyíin
experience xíbra
expert xabíir (xúbara)
to explain fáhhim, yifáhhim
extremely xáaliṣ; lil-gháaya
eye 9een (9uyúun)

f

face wišš (wušúuš)
fact Ha'íi'a (Ha'áayi')
factory máṣna9 (maṣáani9)
faith imáan
to fall wí'i9, yú'a9
family 9éela (9eláat)
famous mašhúur, mašhúura, mašhuríin
fan marwáHa (maráawiH)
far bi9íid, bi9íida, bu9áad
farmer falláaH (fallaHíin)
to fast ṣaam, yiṣúum
fast (*adv.*) bi-súr9a
fasting (*adj.*) ṣáayim, ṣáyma, ṣaymíin
fasting (*n.*) ṣiyáam; ṣoom
fat tixíin, tixíina, tuxáan
father abb (abbaháat)
faucet Hanafíyya (Hanafiyyáat)
to fear xaaf, yixáaf min
fear (*n.*) xoof
feast 9iid (a9yáad)
February fibráayir
few šwáyya
field gheeṭ (ghiṭáan)
film film (afláam)
final niháa'i, niha'íyya, niha'iyyíin
to find lá'a, yiláa'i
fine kwáyyis, kwayyísa, kwayyisíin; **(okay =)** ṭáyyib
finger ṣubáa9 (ṣawáabi9)
to finish xállaṣ, yixállaṣ

fire naar (niráan)
first áwwil; awwaláani, awwalaníyya, awwalaniyyíin
fish sámak (*c.*)
flies ḍibbáan (*c.*)
food akl
foot rigl (rugúul)
for li
forbidden mamnúu9, mamnúu9a, mamnu9íin
foreigner agnábi, agnabíyya, agáanib
to forget nísi, yínsa
France faránsa
freedom Hurríyya
French faransáawi, faransawíyya, faransawiyyíin
Friday yoom ig-gúm9a
fried má'li, ma'líyya, ma'liyyíin
friend ṣáaHib, ṣáHba, aṣHáab
from min
from where? minéen
fruit fákha (fawáakih)
fruitseller fakaháani (fakahaníyya)
full malyáan, malyáana, malyaníin

g

game lí9ba (al9áab)
garbage zibáala
garden ginéena (ganáayin)
garlic toom (*c.*)
gas g̲haaz
gazelle g̲hazáal (g̲hizláan)
generally 9umúuman; 9ála l-9umúum
generosity káram
generous karíim, karíima, kúrama
gentleman xawáaga (xawagáat)
German almáani, almaníyya, almáan
Germany almánya
gift hidíyya (hadáaya)
girl bint (banáat)
to give ídda, yíddi

Giza ig-gíiza
glass 'izáaz; **(drinking =)** kubbáaya (kubbayáat)
to go raaH, yirúuH
God al̤l̤áah
going ráayiH, ráyHa, rayHíin
gold dáhab
good kwáyyis, kwayyísa, kwayyisíin
good (*n.*) xeer
goodbye ma9a s-saláama
government Hukúuma (Hukumáat)
to graduate itxárrag, yitxárrag
grandfather gidd (gudúud)
grandmother gídda (giddáat)
Greece il-yunáan
greed ṭáma9
greedy ṭammáa9, ṭammáa9a, ṭamma9íim
Greek yunáani, yunaníyya, yunaniyyíin; igríigi
green áxḍar, xáḍra, xuḍr
grey ramáadi
grocer ba''áal (ba''alíin)
guest ḍeef (ḍuyúuf)
gulf xalíig (xulgáan)

h

habit 9áada (9adáat)
hair ša9r (*c.*)
half nuṣṣ
hammer šakúuš (šawakíiš)
hand iid (idéen)
handkerchief mandíil (manadíil)
to happen Háṣal, yíHṣal
happy mabsúuṭ, mabsúuṭa, mabsuṭíin
harbour míina (mawáani)
hashiish Hašíiš
he húwwa
head ṛaas (ruus)
headache ṣudáa9
to hear sími9, yísma9

heart 'alb ('ulúub)
heat Harr; Haráara
to heat sáxxan, yisáxxan
heavy ti'íil, ti'íila, tu'áal
to help sáa9id, yisáa9id
help(ing) misá9da
here hína
here is/are ahó, ahé, ahúm
high 9áali, 9álya, 9alyíin
history taríix
to hit ḍárab, yíḍrab
hitting ḍarb
to hold mísik, yímsik
holiday agáaza (agazáat)
home beet (buyúut)
honey 9ásal
to honour šárraf, yišárraf
hope ámal (amáal)
horse Huṣáan (Hiṣína); **horses** xeel (*c.*)
hospital mustášfa (mustašfayáat)
hotel lukánḍa (lukanḍáat)
hour sáa9a (sa9áat)
house beet (buyúut); daar (duur)
how many? kaam
how? izzáay
huge ḍaxm, ḍáxma, ḍuxáam
humidity ruṭúuba
hungry ga9áan, ga9áana, ga9aníin
to hurry istá9gil, yistá9gil
hurrying (*adj.*) mistá9gil, mista9gíla, mista9gilíin
husband gooz (agwáaz)

i

I ána
ice talg
ice cream žiláati
idea fíkra (afkáar)

idiot 9abíiṭ, 9abíiṭa, 9ubṭ
if in; íza; law
to imagine itṣáwwar, yitṣáwwar
immediately 9ála ṭuul
important muhímm, muhímma, muhimmíin
impossible miš múmkin
to improve (*tr.*) Hássin, yiHássin; (*intr.*) itHássin, yitHássin
improvement (*tr.*) taHsíin
in fi, gúwwa
in front of 'uddáam
industry ṣináa9a (ṣina9áat)
inexpensive rixíiṣ, rixíiṣa, ruxáaṣ
influence nufúuz
inhabitant sáakin (sukkáan)
ink Hibr
to inquire istá9lim, yistá9lim 9an
inquiries isti9lamáat
inside gúwwa; dáaxil
instead bádal; bádal ma + *v.*
intelligent záki, zakíyya, ázkiya
to intend náwa, yínwi
interested in muhtámm, muhtámma, muhtammíin bi
interesting **(enjoyable =)** múmti9, mumtí9a, mumti9íin; **(exciting =)** musíir
interpreter mutárgim (mutargimíin)
to invite 9ázam, yí9zim 9ála
Iraq il-9iráa'
Iraqi 9iráa'i, 9ira'íyya, 9ira'iyyíin
to iron káwa, yíkwi
iron (substance =) Hadíid; **(for laundry =)** mákwa (makáawi)
to irrigate ráwa, yírwi
irrigation rayy
Islam isláam
Islamic isláami, islamíyya, islamiyyíin
island gizíira (gúzur)
Israel isra'íil
it húwwa (*m.*); híyya (*f.*)
Italy iṭálya
ivory 9aag

j

jam mirábba (mirabbáat)
January yanáayir
Jew(ish) yahúudi, yahudíyya, yahúud
job šug͟hl (ašg͟háal)
joke núkta (núkat)
journalist ṣúHafi, ṣuHafíyya, ṣuHafiyyíin
journey ríHla (riHláat); sáfar (asfáar)
joy fáraH
judgement Hukm
juice 9aṣíir
July yúlyu
June yúnyu

k

key muftáaH (mafatíiH)
to kill máwwit, yimáwwit; (**murder** =) 'átal, yí'til
kilogram kíilu (kiluháat)
kind (sort =) noo9 (anwáa9)
king málik (mulúuk)
kitchen máṭbax (maṭáabix)
knife sikkíina (sakakíin)
to know 9íri9, yí9rif
knowing 9áarif, 9árfa, 9arfíin
Koran il-qur'áan

l

lady sitt (sitáat)
lame á9rag, 9árga, 9urg
land arḍ (aráaḍi); barr
language lúg͟ha (lug͟háat)
large kibíir, kibíira, kubáar
last áaxir; axíir, axíira; axráani, axraníyya, axraniyyíin
late wáxri, waxríyya, waxriyyíin; mit'áxxar, mit'axxára, mit'axxaríin
later ba9déen

to laugh ḍíHik, yíḍHak

laughter ḍiHk

laundryman makwági (makwagíyya)

law qanúun (qawaníin)

lawyer muHáami (muHamíin)

lazy kasláan, kasláana, kaslaníin

to learn it9állim, yit9állim

leather gild (gulúud)

Lebanon libnáan

lecture muHáḍra (muHaḍráat)

left šimáal

leg rigl (*f.*)

lemons lamúun (*c.*)

length ṭuul

lentils 9ads

lesson dars (durúus)

letter gawáab (gawabáat)

lettuce xaṣṣ (*c.*)

liberation taHríir

library maktába (maktabáat)

lift aṣanṣéer (aṣanṣeráat)

light (*n.*) nuur

light(-weight) xafíif, xafíifa, xufáaf

to like Habb, yiHíbb

like zayy

to listen sími9, yísma9

little (small =) sugháyyar, sughayyára, sughayyaríin; **(a little =)** šwáyya

to live (inhabit =) sákan, yúskun

living sáakin, sákna, sakníin

local maHálli, maHalíyya, maHalliyyíin; báladi

London lándan

long ṭawíil, ṭawíila, ṭuwáal

to look (at) baṣṣ, yibúṣṣ li

lover Habíib, Habíiba, Habáayib

luck baxt

lunch gháda

to lunch itghádda, yitghádda

Luxor lú'ṣur

m

magazine magálla (magalláat)
maid šaghgháala (šaghghaláat)
mail búṣṭa; baríid
mailman buṣṭági (buṣṭagíyya)
majority aghlabíyya
man ṛáagil (riggáala)
manager mudíir (mudiríin)
mangoes mánga (*c.*)
many kitíir
map xaríiṭa (xaṛáayiṭ)
March máaris
market suu' (aswáa')
marriage gawáaz
married mitgáwwiz, mitgawwíza, mitgawwizíin
matches kabríit
mathematics riyáaḍa
May máayu
meat láHma
mechanic mikaníiki (mikanikíyya)
medicine dáwa (m.) (ádwiya)
to meet (*tr.*) 'áabil, yi'áabil; (*intr.*) it'áabil, yit'áabil
meeting igtimáa9
merchandise biḍáa9a (baḍáayi9)
merchant táagir (tuggáar)
Middle East iš-šarq il-áwsaṭ
minister wazíir (wúzara)
ministry wizáara (wizaráat)
minus ílla
minute di'íi'a (da'áayi')
mirror miráaya (mirayáat)
miser baxíil, baxíila, búxula
Miss aanísa (anisáat)
miss (lit.: to be missed by =) wáHaš, yíwHaš
mistake ghálṭa (ghalṭáat)
Monday yoom il-itnéen
money filúus
month šahr (ašhur or šuhúur)

moon 'ámar
Moslem múslim, muslíma, muslimíin
mosque gáami9 (gawáami9)
mosquitoes namúus (*c.*)
mother umm (ummaháat); wálda (waldáat)
mouse faar (firáan)
mouth bu''; Hának
Mr is-sáyyid
Mrs is-sitt; madáam
much kitíir
to muddle láxbaṭ, yiláxbaṭ
municipality baladíyya
museum mátHaf (matáaHif)
music musíiqa

n

name ism (asáami)
napkin fúuṭa (fúwaṭ)
narrow dáyya', dayyá'a, dayya'íin
nation dáwla (dúwal)
national wáṭani, waṭaníyya, waṭaniyyíin; qáwmi, qawmíyya, qawmiyyíin; áhli, ahlíyya, ahliyyíin
nationality ginsíyya (ginsiyyáat)
native (*adj.*) báladi
near 'uráyyib, 'urayyíba, 'urayyibíin
necessary ḍarúuri
necktie karavátta (karavattáat)
to need iHtáag, yiHtáag li
neighbour gaar (giráan)
neither . . . nor la . . . wála
never ábadan
new gidíid, gidiida, gudáad
news xábar (axbáar)
newspaper gurnáan (garaníin)
night léela (layáali); leel
Nile in-niil
no la'
nobody maHáddiš

noon ḍuhr
north šamáal
not miš
notebook kuṛṛáasa (kaṛaríis)
nothing wála Háaga
November nufímbir
now dilwá'ti
nowhere wála Hítta
number 9add (a9dáad); nímra (nímar)

o

O . . . (*voc.*) ya
occasion munásba (munasbáat)
occupied mašg̲h̲úul, mašg̲h̲úula, mašg̲h̲ulíin
October uktúubar
of bitáa9, bitá9t, bitúu9
of course ṭáb9an
to offer 'áddim, yi'áddim
office máktab (makáatib)
often kitíir
oil zeet (zuyúut); (**petroleum =**) bitróol
old 'adíim, 'adíima, 'udáam
olives zatúun (*c.*)
on 9ála
once máṛṛa
one-eyed á9war, 9óora, 9uur
onion báṣal (*c.*)
only bass
to open fátaH, yíftaH
open (*adj.*) maftúuH, maftúuHa, maftuHíin
operation 9amalíyya (9amaliyyáat)
opinion ra'y (aráa')
opportunity fúrṣa (fúraṣ)
or aw; wálla
orange (colour) burtu'áani
orange (fruit) burtu'áan (*c.*)
to order (ask for =) ṭálab, yúṭlub
ordinary 9áadi, 9adíyya, 9adiyyíin

to organize náẓẓam, yináẓẓam
organized munáẓẓam, munaẓẓáma, munaẓẓamíin
origin aṣl (uṣúul)
other táani, tánya, tanyíin
out of order 9aṭláan, 9aṭláana, 9aṭlaníin
outing fúsHa (fúsaH)
outside bárra
oven furn (afráan)
over foo'
overcoat bálṭu (baláaṭi)
owner ṣáaHib (aṣHáab)

p

to pack (suitcases =) wáḍḍab, yiwáḍḍab
page ṣáfHa (ṣafHáat)
pain wága9 (awgáa9)
paint búuya (buyáat)
palace 'aṣr ('uṣúur)
paper wára'
party Háfla (Hafláat)
pasha báaša (bašawáat)
to pass faat, yifúut; marr, yimúrr
passenger ráakib (rukkáab)
passport gawáaz sáfar (gawazáat sáfar)
patience ṣabr
to pay dáfa9, yídfa9
paying daf9 (*v.n.*)
peace saláam
peanuts fuul sudáani
peas bisílla (*c.*)
peasant falláaH, falláaHa, fallaHíin
pedestrians mušáa
pen 'álam (a'láam)
people naas
perhaps yímkin
period múdda (múdad)
permission izn
to permit sámaH, yísmaH

personally šaxsíyyan
pessimist(ic) mutašáa'im, mutašaá'ima, mutaša'imíin
petrol benzíin
petroleum bitróol
Pharaoh far9óon (fará9na)
Pharaonic far9óoni, far9oníyya, far9oniyyíin
pharmacy agzaxáana (agzaxanáat)
photograph ṣúura (ṣúwar)
piaster 'irš ('urúuš)
picture ṣúura (ṣúwar)
piece Hítta (Hítat)
pigeons Hamáam (*c.*)
pilgrim Hagg (Huggáag)
pilgrimage Higg; **(to go on pilgrimage =)** Hagg, yiHígg
pipe (to smoke) bíiba (bibáat)
poetry ši9r
police bulíis
policeman 9askári (9asáakir)
polite mu'áddab, mu'addába, mu'addabíin
poor fa'íir, fa'íira, fú'ara
port míina (mawáani)
porter šayyáal (šayyalíin)
possible múmkin
post baríid; búṣṭa
post office máktab baríid
postman buṣṭági (buṣṭagíyya)
potatoes baṭáaṭis (*c.*)
pound (£) ginéeh (gineháat)
to pray ṣálla, yiṣálli
to prefer fáḍḍal, yifáḍḍal
to prepare Háḍḍar, yiHáḍḍar
president ra'íis (rú'asa)
to prevent mána9, yímna9
price si9r (as9áar)
problem muškíla (mašáakil)
programme birnáamig (baráamig)
progress ta'áddum
proverb másal (amsáal)
put Haṭṭ, yiHúṭṭ
pyramid háram (ahráam or ahramáat)

q

quarter rub9
question su’áal (as’íla)
queue ṭabúur (ṭawabíir)
quickly bi-súr9a

r

rabbit árnab (aráanib)
radio rádyu (radyuháat)
rain máṭar
to rain maṭṭárit, timáṭṭar
to read ’ara, yi’ra
ready musta9ídd, musta9ídda, musta9iddíin li
real Ha’íi’i, Ha’i’íyya, Ha’i’iyyíin
reasonable ma9’úul
to receive istálam, yistílim
red áHmar, Hámra, Humr
refrigerator talláaga (tallagáat)
relation 9iláa’a (9ila’áat)
relatively nisbíyyan
religion diin (adyáan)
religious diini, diníyya, diniyyíin
remaining báa’i
to renew gáddid, yigáddid
to rent ággar, yi’ággar; (*n.*) **rent** igaar
to repair ṣállaH, yiṣállaH
republic gumhuríyya (gumhuriyyáat)
research baHs
reservation Hagz
to reserve Hágaz, yíHgiz
to reside sákan, yúskun
to resign ista’áal, yista’íil
resignation isti’áala (isti’aláat)
to respect iHtáram, yiHtírim; (*n.*) **respect** iHtiraam
restaurant máṭ9am (maṭáa9im)
to ride ríkib, yírkab
right (-hand side =) yimíin

ring xáatim (xawáatim)
to rise (get **up** =) 'aam, yi'úum
river nahr (anháar)
river-bank ḍáffa (ḍifáaf)
road ṭaríi' (ṭúru')
room óḍa (ówaḍ)
to run gíri, yígri
Russia rúsya
Russian rúusi, rusíyya, ruus

s

safety saláama
sailor baHHáar
salad ṣálaṭa (ṣalaṭáat)
same nafs
Saturday yoom is-sábt
Saudi Arabia is-su9udíyya
schedule gádwal (gadáawil)
school madrása (madáaris)
science 9ilm (9ulúum)
sea baHr (biHáar)
season faṣl (fuṣúul)
second sánya (sawáani)
secondary school madrása sanawíyya
secret sirr (asráar)
to see šaaf, yišúuf
seeing šáayif, šayfa, šayfíin
self nafs
to sell baa9, yibíi9
seller bayyáa9 (bayya9íin)
selling bee9 (*v.n.*)
to send bá9at, yíb9at
sentence gúmla (gúmal)
September sibtímbir
serious gadd (*invariable*)
servant xaddáam (xaddamíin)
service xídma
to shave Hála', yíHla'

she híyya
shelf raff (rufúuf)
ship márkib (maráakib); báaxira (bawáaxir)
shirt 'amíiṣ ('umṣáan)
shoe (pair of =) gázma (gízam)
shop maHáll (maHalláat)
short 'uṣáyyar, 'uṣayyára, 'uṣayyaríin
to show wárra, yiwárri
sick 9ayyáan, 9ayyáana, 9ayyaníin
silver fáḍḍa
sing g͟hánna, yig͟hánni
sister uxt (ixwáat)
to sit 'á9ad, yú'9ud
sitting 'áa9id, 'á9da, 'a9díin
sky sáma
to sleep naam, yináam
sleeping náayim, náyma, naymíin
slowly bi-šwéeš
small ṣug͟háyyar, ṣug͟hayyára, ṣug͟hayyaríin
to smell šamm, yišímm
to smoke šírib, yíšrib (sagáayir)
smoke (*n.*) duxxáan
smoking tadxíin
soldier 9askári (9asáakir)
some ba9ḍ
sometimes aHyáanan
son ibn (awláad or wiláad)
to speak itkállim, yitkállim
specially xuṣúuṣan
speech kaláam
speed súr9a (sur9áat)
spoon ma9lá'a (ma9áali')
sports riyáaḍa
spring ir-rabíi9
square (city-square =) midáan (mayadíin)
stamp (postage =) ṭáabi9 (ṭawáabi9)
to stand wí'if, yú'af
station maHáṭṭa (maHaṭṭáat)
to steal sára', yísra'

steam buxáar
still líssa
stomach baṭn (*f.*)
stopping wáa'if, wá'fa, wa'fíin
straight dúghri
street šáari9 (šawáari9)
student (*m.*) ṭáalib (ṭulláab or ṭálaba); (*f.*) ṭaalíba (ṭaalibáat)
to study dáras, yídris; záakir, yizáakir
success nagáaH
sugar súkkar
suit bádla (bídal)
suitcase (bag=) šánṭa (šúnaṭ)
summer iṣ-ṣeef
sun šams
Sunday yoom il-Hádd
sure muta'ákkid, muta'akkída, muta'akkidíin
sweet Hilw, Hílwa, Hilwíin
to swim 9aam, yi9úum; síbiH, yísbaH
system niẓáam (ánzima)

t

table ṭaṛabéeza (ṭaṛabezáat)
tailor ṭárzi (ṭarzíyya)
to take xad, yáaxud
to talk itkállim, yitkállim
tall ṭawíil, ṭawíila, ṭuwáal
to taste daa', yidúu'
tea šaay
to teach dárris, yidárris; 9állim, yi9állim
teacher mudárris, mudarrísa, mudarrisíin; mu9állim, mu9allíma, mu9allimíin
to tease 9áakis, yi9áakis
technical fánni, fanníyya, fanniyyíin
telephone tilifóon (tilifonáat)
television tilfizyóon (tilfizyunáat)
to tell 'aal, yiúul li
test imtiHáan (imtiHanáat)
thank you šúkran

theatre másraH (masáariH)
then bá'a
there hináak
there is fiih
they húmma
thief Haráami (Haramíyya)
thin rufáyya9, rufayyá9a, rufayya9íin
thing Háaga (Hagáat)
to think fákkar, yifákkar; iftákar, yiftíkir
third tilt
thirsty 9aṭšáan, 9aṭšáana, 9aṭšaníin
this, that da, di, dool
to throw ráma, yírmi
Thursday yoom il-xamíis
ticket tazkára (tazáakir)
to tie rábaṭ, yúrbuṭ
tiles baláaṭ (*c.*)
time wa't
time(s) maṛṛa (maṛṛáat)
tired ta9báan, ta9báana, ta9baníin
title 9inwáan (9anawíin)
today innahárda
together sáwa, má9a ba9ḍ
tomatoes 'úuṭa (*c.*); ṭamaaṭim
tomorrow búkra
tonight il-léela
too kamáan
towel fúuṭa (fúwaṭ)
tower borg (burúug)
town bálad (biláad)
traffic murúur
train 'aṭr ('uṭuráat)
to translate tárgim, yitárgim
translation targáma (targamáat)
translator mutárgim (mutargimíin)
to travel sáafir, yisáafir
travel sáfar
traveller misáafir
trees šágar (*c.*)

trip ríHla (riHláat)
trousers banṭalóon (banṭalonáat)
to try Háawil, yiHáawil
Tuesday yoom it-taláat
turkey diik rúumi
Turkey turkíiya
Turkish túrki, turkíyya, atráak

u

unbelievable miš ma9'úul
under taHt
to understand fíhim, yífham
understanding fahm; (**mutual understanding** =) ṭafáahum
understanding fáahim, fáhma, fahmíin
United Kingdom il-mamláka l-muttáHida
United States il-wilayáat il-muttáHida
university gám9a (gam9áat)
until lighāayit
Upper Egypt iṣ-ṣi9íid
to use istá9mil, yistá9mil
use (benefit =) fáyda
used to (accustomed =) mit9áwwid, mit9awwída, mit9awwidíin
useful mufíid, mufíida, mufidíin
usually 9aadátan; fil-9áada

v

vacation agáaza (agazáat)
valley wáadi (widyáan)
Valley of the Kings wáadi l-mulúuk
veal bitíllu
vegetables xuḍáar
very gíddan; 'áwi
villa vílla (vílal)
village qárya (qúra)
visit ziyáara (ziyaráat)
to visit zaar, yizúur
visit ziyáara
voice ṣoot (aṣwáat)

w

wanting 9áawiz; 9áayiz
war Harb (Hurúub)
we íHna
weak ḍa'íif, ḍa'íifa, ḍu'áaf
to wear líbis, yílbis
weather gaww
wedding fáraH (afráaH)
Wednesday yoom il-árba9
week usbúu9 (asabíi9)
to weep 9áyyaṭ, yi9áyyaṭ
weight wazn
welcome áhlan wa sáhlan
well biir (abáar)
well (*adv.*) kwáyyis
west g̲harb
what? eeh
where? feen
white ábyaḍ, béeḍa, biiḍ
who? miin
why? leeh
wife sitt (sitáat); miṛáat (+ *n./pron.*)
window šibbáak (šababíik)
wine nibíit
winter iš-šíta
with má9a
without bidúun; min g̲heer
woman sitt (sitáat)
wood xášab
wool ṣuuf
word kílma (kilmáat)
to work ištág̲hal, yištág̲hal
work šug̲hl
worker 9áamil (9ummáal)
world dínya
to write kátab, yíktib
writer káatib, kátba, kuttáab
wrong (in error =) g̲halṭáan, g̲halṭáana, g̲halṭaníin

y

year sána (siníin)
yellow áṣfar, ṣáfra, ṣufr
yes áywa
yesterday imbáariH
yet líssa
you (*f.*) ínti
you (*m.*) ínta
you (*pl.*) íntu